THE ULTIMATE PRACTICAL GUIDE TO
SCRAPBOOKING

THE ULTIMATE PRACTICAL GUIDE TO
SCRAPBOOKING

CREATING FABULOUS LASTING
MEMORY JOURNALS TO CHERISH

contributing editor: Alison Lindsay

HERMES
HOUSE

This edition is published by Hermes House
an imprint of Anness Publishing Ltd
Hermes House, 88–89 Blackfriars Road
London SE1 8HA
tel. 020 7401 2077; fax 020 7633 9499

www.hermeshouse.com; www.annesspublishing.com

If you like the images in this book and would like to investigate using
them for publishing, promotions or advertising, please visit our website
www.practicalpictures.com for more information.

Publisher: Joanna Lorenz
Editorial Director: Helen Sudell
Editors: Ann Kay and Simona Hill
Designer: Terry Jeavons
Photographers: Mark Wood and Paul Bricknell
Editorial Reader: Emily Adenipekun
Production Controller: Steve Lang

ETHICAL TRADING POLICY
At Anness Publishing we believe that business should be conducted in an
ethical and ecologically sustainable way, with respect for the environment
and a proper regard to the replacement of the natural resources we employ.
As a publisher, we use a lot of wood pulp to make high-quality paper for
printing, and that wood commonly comes from spruce trees. We are
therefore currently growing more than 500,000 trees in two Scottish forest
plantations near Aberdeen – Berrymoss (130 hectares/320 acres) and West
Touxhill (125 hectares/305 acres). The forests we manage contain twice the
number of trees employed each year in paper-making for our books.
Because of this ongoing ecological investment programme, you, as our
customer, can have the pleasure and reassurance of knowing that a tree is
being cultivated on your behalf to naturally replace the materials used to
make the book you are holding.
   Our forestry programme is run in accordance with the UK Woodland
Assurance Scheme (UKWAS) and will be certified by the internationally
recognized Forest Stewardship Council (FSC). The FSC is a non-government
organization dedicated to promoting responsible management of the world's
forests. Certification ensures forests are managed in an environmentally
sustainable and socially responsible way. For further information about this
scheme, go to www.annesspublishing.com/trees

CONTENTS

INTRODUCTION

In the early days of photography, having a picture taken was a notable event. It generally involved a visit to a professional photographer's studio, and the resulting prints – though they might be small and hard to see in tones of sepia or grey – were treasured and displayed in silver frames or ornate albums. Now we live in an age where photography is all around us. It is easier than ever before to take beautiful, detailed, interesting photographs whenever we want, and yet many good prints languish in boxes or drawers. The burgeoning craft of scrapbooking is all about displaying them as they deserve to be seen. But scrapbooks are more than just photograph albums: on their pages you can present your favourite pictures in beautiful, creative settings, accompanied by all the details you need to keep your memories of special times alive and fresh, to enjoy now and to pass down to future generations.

This comprehensive guide includes everything you need to get you started, whatever your artistic ability, with practical tips and inspiring suggestions for pages of originality and style. The opening

▼ *Christmas is a good subject for scrapbooks and there is always plenty of decorative material to hand.*

▲ *Old black-and-white photographs show how times change when compared to today's colour prints.*

section details the different kinds of materials and equipment you can choose from to make your pages and sets out easy techniques for mounting and editing photographs, creating backgrounds and making decorations. It also explores a range of styles and shows how to achieve each look. In the second part of the book, 120 step-by-step projects put the basic techniques into practice, with inspirational results. They are grouped around popular themes such as Children, Weddings, Travel and Family History, to help you decide how to organize your own collections.

Before you begin work on your first page, you need to decide on the size of the album you will use, as this will dictate the size of the layout. Most of the projects in this book are based on 30cm/12in square pages, on which there is plenty of space to mount a good selection of pictures and embellish them creatively. Scrapbooking suppliers offer a huge range of paper, card and other materials in this popular size. Alternatively, you could go for the slightly smaller 21 x 28cm/8½ x 11in. This has the advantage that you can print material on A4 paper to fit it, but it can be more difficult to arrange all the items you want on a single page or double-page spread. Smaller size albums are also available, such as 20cm/8in square, and can be useful if you want to create mini-albums as gifts. Of course, you can also make your own albums and covers in any size you wish, and there are some great ideas in this book for displaying your designs in one-off albums and other unusual ways.

Albums use a number of different binding systems: with three-ring bindings it is easy to move pages around, but they hold a limited number of pages, and the rings make it difficult to display double-page layouts effectively. This is not a problem with post-bound or strap-bound albums, which can expand to take more pages as your collection grows. Whatever you choose, always look for albums and papers that are of "archival" quality, made with acid-free and lignin-free materials, so that your precious prints don't deteriorate once they are mounted.

Like many other aspects of life, the digital revolution plays a vital part in many areas of scrapbooking. Digital cameras and image-editing software have opened up all kinds of photographic possibilities. With no need to buy film, you can take as

▼ *Children are a perennially popular subject for scrapbooks, and children will love looking at their own photographs.*

▲ *Photographs of a family trip to the seaside take on a nostalgic appearance when embellished with 1950s memorabilia.*

many experimental pictures as you like and play around with novel formats, colour and special effects. An internet connection gives you access to online craft suppliers, sources of templates and fonts, and special interest groups with whom you can discuss your projects and display your favourites in virtual galleries. There is now a growing trend towards virtual scrapbooking, in which stickers, borders and charms are replaced by digital versions entirely assembled and displayed on screen.

However, it's certainly not necessary to have a computer in order to enjoy scrapbooking to the full. This craft's great attraction derives from the fact that it is a wonderfully back-to-basics pastime. Good layouts combine artistic flair with genuine hands-on skills with paper, card, fabrics and natural materials. Like the quilting and knitting bees of previous generations, communal scrapbooking events (known as "crops") are strengthening social networks everywhere. As you trim, glue and assemble the elements of your pages, you can rediscover all the enthusiasm and satisfaction you felt when compiling a scrapbook as a child, in the knowledge that you are safeguarding and enhancing your treasured family memorabilia for your own children and for future generations.

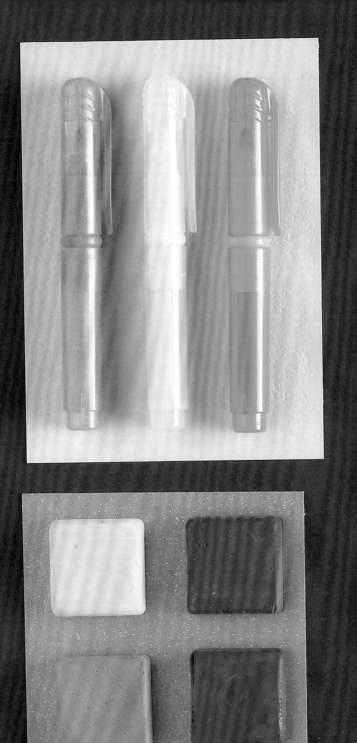
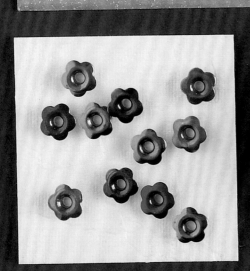

Getting started

Creating album pages is about encapsulating life's precious moments in a way that feels right for you. As you gain experience you'll have plenty of ideas for presentation and develop your own personal style. There are lots of ways to make exciting scrapbooks, and there are tips to guide you through your ideas to help you make the best of irreplaceable prints and memorabilia.

   Craft stores are bursting with seductive pieces of kit and decorative materials, and it's very easy to get carried away buying stickers, die stamps and fancy cutters that appeal to your sense of colour and style before you have any clear idea of what you'll do with them. This section offers a guide to the materials and equipment available, to help you match the possibilities to the items you want to display. Step-by-step instructions will take you through all the different photographic and craft techniques you need to make beautiful, meaningful pages.

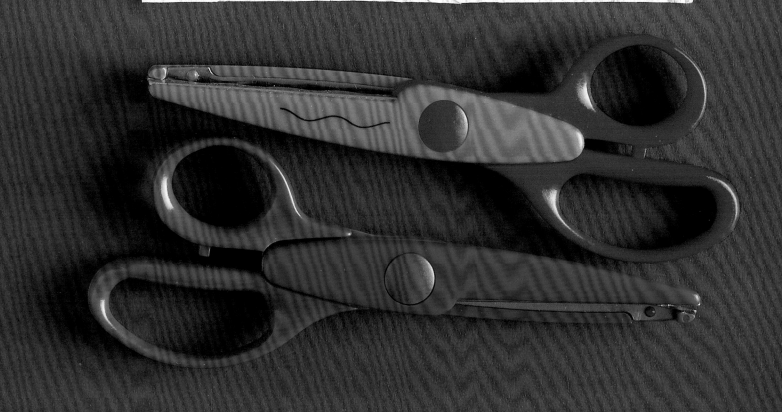

EQUIPMENT AND MATERIALS

It's easy to get carried away by the vast range of fancy punches, stamps and stickers available for scrapbooking. Start with the basics – album pages, scissors and adhesive – and add to your collection gradually as you develop your themes.

Cutting tools

Whatever the style of your albums, impeccably accurate cutting is essential for good-looking results. Bad trimming can ruin your precious pictures, so invest in good scissors and knives.

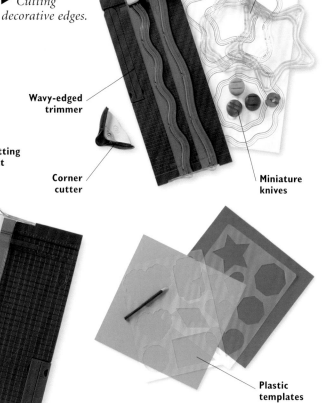

▶ *Cutting decorative edges.*

Template sheets

Shaped plastic templates

Wavy-edged trimmer

Corner cutter

Miniature knives

Metal ruler and craft knife

These give total control over where and how you cut. The knife blade should always be retracted or covered when not in use. If safety is a concern, a guillotine or trimmer may be a better option.

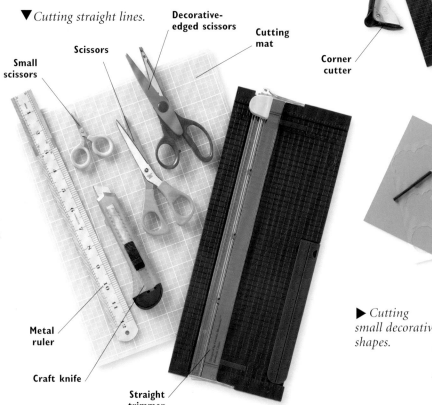

▼ *Cutting straight lines.*

Decorative-edged scissors

Cutting mat

Scissors

Small scissors

Metal ruler

Craft knife

Straight trimmer

Straight trimmer or guillotine

Use this to trim paper or photographs with straight edges. All trimmers have a grid printed or embossed on to the cutting surface, to help you measure accurately. Some have interchangeable blades that cut patterned lines as well as straight ones.

Plastic templates

▶ *Cutting small decorative shapes.*

Punches

Speciality cutters

There are all kinds of cutters available that make it easy to cut photographs and mats into decorative shapes. Placing a template over a photograph allows you to see what size to cut. Templates and cutters are only suitable for use together.

Templates

A wide range of lightweight templates provide different cropping options, and are easy to store. Use a pencil with the template to trace a shape on to a photograph or paper, then cut along the drawn line with scissors.

Punches

Simple small shapes look striking when punched in coloured card. Larger shapes can also be used to cut out the important part of a photograph. Shaped punches are available in hundreds of designs, and can be combined for added impact: for example, several hearts can be assembled together to create the petals of a flower.

Scissors

It is useful to have two pairs of scissors: a large pair for cutting straight lines and a small pair for trimming around decorative shapes and templates. Blades with pointed tips make it easier to cut out intricate shapes.

Decorative-edged scissors

Used sparingly, these add a fancy touch to mats and trims, although it is advisable not to use them on photographs. They work best when cutting a straight edge or a gentle curve.

Guillotine

Adhesives

Many different kinds of adhesive will work well on paper and card (card stock). Make sure any you use are labelled acid-free so that your photographs will not deteriorate when in contact with them.

Glue sticks

These are a cheap and easy way to stick light items such as punched shapes, but some glue sticks are not strong enough to hold photographs in position permanently. Although the glue takes some time to dry, it does not need to be left flat while drying.

Spray adhesive

Both permanent and repositionable adhesives are available in spray form – the latter allows for something that is stuck down to be peeled off and then reapplied. Spray outside or in a well-ventilated room, so that the fumes can disperse. To prevent the spray going everywhere, it is a good idea to place items in a large box, and direct the spray into that. No drying time is required.

Foam pads

These can be used to raise an element on a layout, making it appear three-dimensional. For greater height, you can stick two or more pads together before mounting your item. Use scissors to trim the pads if they are too large, but clean the scissor blades afterwards.

Glue dots and glue lines

These are available in different sizes and thicknesses, and with permanent or repositionable adhesive. The glue is tacky and will hold most items securely. No drying time is required.

Double-sided tape

Whether as a single sheet, pre-cut into squares, or on a continuous roll, this is a clean, easy way to glue most items. Long strips can be used to created borders, by applying a piece of tape, removing the backing, then pouring beads or glitter over the exposed tape. Use the same technique with small shapes punched from a sheet. No drying time is required.

Tape applicators

These dispensers allow for the convenient application of a square or line of adhesive, making it easy to glue the edge of unusual or angled shapes.

Refills are available for most designs, making them economical too. No drying time is required.

PVA (white) glue

This will hold most items in place, including awkward or three-dimensional items such as shells or charms. The work must be left flat while the glue dries. To cover an album or box, brush glue diluted with water over a sheet of paper and wrap it around the sides.

Photo corners

If you prefer to avoid gluing your photographs permanently, mount them with photo corners. Because the adhesive is on the corner and not the photograph, the picture can be removed later if necessary. Clear photo corners are the most useful, but coloured ones are also available. Gold, silver or black look good on heritage or wedding layouts. No drying time is required.

Masking tape

This is useful for temporarily attaching stencils to a layout, or for lifting stickers from their backing sheet.

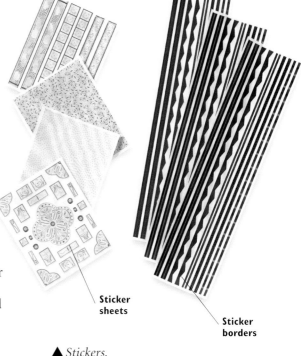

Sticker sheets

Sticker borders

▲ *Stickers.*

Glue for vellum

Specially made "invisible" glue dots are needed when working with vellum, to avoid the adhesive showing through the sheet. Alternatively, it can be attached using spray adhesive.

Stickers

As well as being a decorative element, stickers can be positioned to attach vellum, photographs or journaling blocks to a layout. Choose large scale stickers if you want to stick a heavy item down.

▼ *Adhesive materials.*

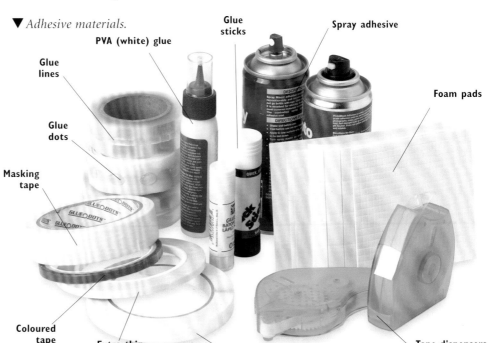

Glue sticks

Spray adhesive

PVA (white) glue

Glue lines

Glue dots

Masking tape

Foam pads

Coloured tape

Extra-thin tape

Double-sided tape

Tape dispensers

Paper and card

Good paper makes a world of difference to your designs, so always buy the best quality you can afford, and make sure it is acid-free to keep your photographs in perfect condition.

Page kits
Sometimes helpful for beginners, page kits combine paper with matching stickers or other embellishments and offer an easy way to create co-ordinated layouts quickly. They are designed to suit a range of themes and cover many different subjects.

Self-coloured card (stock)
This is the basis for many scrapbook pages, and its firmness provides an ideal surface to support photographs and embellishments. Card may be smooth or textured to resemble natural surfaces such as linen. It is available from art and craft suppliers, as single sheets or in multi-packs. Save scraps for paper piecing and matting photos.

Patterned paper
There are thousands of patterned papers available to match almost any theme, event or mood. Papers may be purchased individually, in books or multi-packs; the latter offer better value, but not all the sheets may be to your taste. A folder of patterned paper scraps is useful since many layouts can be attractively embellished using small scraps of paper.

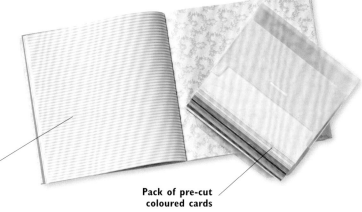

▶ *Mini-album materials.*

Blank notebook

Pack of pre-cut coloured cards

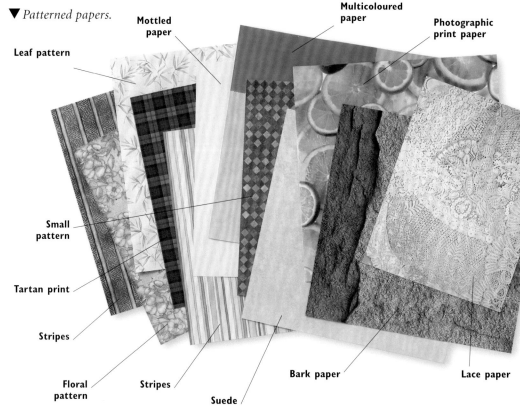

▼ *Patterned papers.*

Mottled paper

Leaf pattern

Multicoloured paper

Photographic print paper

Small pattern

Tartan print

Stripes

Floral pattern

Stripes

Suede paper

Bark paper

Lace paper

▼ *Self-coloured card.*

Glitter card

Textured and embossed paper
These tactile papers give a design texture and depth without adding bulk. Some papers resemble leather or fabric, while others have stitching or metallic embossing to add richness.

Mulberry paper
The fibres used to create this paper are light but very strong. Do not use scissors to cut the paper; instead, "draw" a damp paintbrush across the paper, then tear apart, leaving soft, feathery edges.

Photographic print paper
Some patterned papers offer photographic or naturalistic representations of everyday objects. These can overwhelm a layout if they compete with your own photographs, so restrict them to accents.

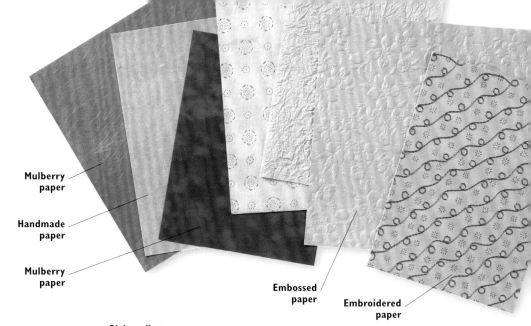

Textured and embossed papers.

Mulberry paper

Handmade paper

Mulberry paper

Embossed paper

Embroidered paper

Suede paper
This mimics the texture and appearance of real suede, and so is perfect for representing that material.

Glitter and pearlescent paper
The soft sheen of pearlescent paper is ideal for baby or wedding layouts, while brighter glitter sheets can be used as colourful accents for party pages.

Cut and mini-album packs
Pre-cut small paper packs are available for matting or mini-albums.

Lace papers
These delicate papers mimic the soft colours and patterns of lace without adding weight to the pages, and are perfect for wedding or heritage layouts.

Vellum
Being translucent, vellum gives a soft look to paper or photographs placed underneath it. Patterned vellum can be layered over plain or patterned paper to create a romantic look, and mini-envelopes made from vellum half-conceal the souvenirs they hold. If a photograph you want to use is a little out of focus, you can disguise this by slipping it behind vellum.

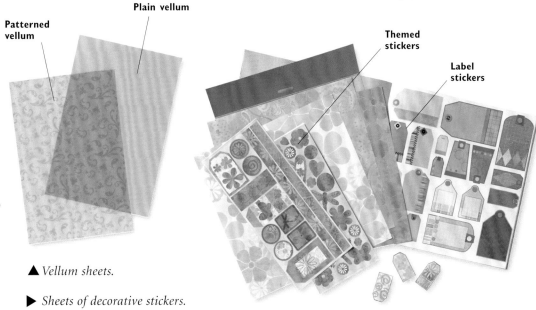

Patterned vellum

Plain vellum

Themed stickers

Label stickers

▲ *Vellum sheets.*

▶ *Sheets of decorative stickers.*

ALBUM BINDINGS

Your album can be of any size, but you will probably find that a 30cm/12in square format offers the best scope for creating satisfying layouts. Loose-leaf albums give the most flexibility, and there are basically three methods of binding pages into them.

Ring binder albums
These are the cheapest way to display layouts, which can be slipped into clear plastic page protectors. Extra page protectors can be added to expand the album. As the ring binding lies between the two pages and distracts the eye, ring binders are best used to present single-page layouts.

Post-bound albums
These albums conceal the posts binding the page protectors together, so a double layout can be viewed without distracting elements. They are available in a wide range of sizes and designs. Extra page protectors may be inserted by unscrewing the posts and adding extenders.

Strap-hinge albums
Plastic hinges slide through loops on the spines of these album pages to create an infinitely extendable album. Each page is an integral part of this kind of album, so background paper needs to be glued on top (known as "wallpapering") to change the layout base.

Notebooks
Any kind of notebook may be used as a scrapbook, especially if a smaller gift album is being created. Decorate plain notebooks by painting or covering with paper, and add embellishments for a unique look. Don't forget to leave room for a title page before the first layout.

Embellishments

This is where the fun really starts, but it's important to keep the focus of attention on your own photographs and memorabilia: make sure the decorative elements enhance the theme of your page rather than dominate it.

▶ *Stickers and adhesive borders.*

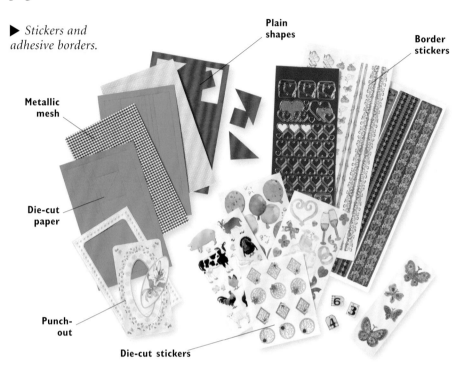

Metallic mesh

Die-cut paper

Punch-out

Die-cut stickers

Plain shapes

Border stickers

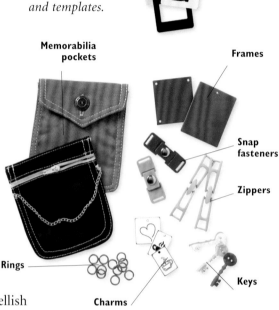

Multi-shape template

Adhesive mesh strip

Slide mounts

▶ *Photo mounts and templates.*

Memorabilia pockets

Frames

Snap fasteners

Zippers

Keys

Charms

Rings

▲ *Fabric pockets and attachments add interest to a layout.*

Stickers

A staple of scrapbooking, stickers are available in every conceivable colour, size and design, and make it easy to embellish a page quickly. Popular characters are represented on stickers, as well as traditional themes such as Christmas and weddings. If you want to make a sticker more substantial, apply it to white card and cut round it, then mount the shape on a foam pad.

Fabric stickers

These are printed on fabric to add textural interest to a layout. For a homespun look, fray some of the threads at the edges of the sticker.

3D stickers

These are built up from two or more layers of card, ready to be added to a page. Popular themes include babies and travel, and many are also suitable for making greetings cards.

Punch-outs

Shapes die-cut from sheets of card are known as punch-outs, as they need to be pressed out of the backing sheet. They are usually simple shapes, and may be coloured. Printed

shapes, or those carrying titles, embellish a layout quickly, and can create a consistent style throughout an album.

Stamping

Use stamps to create a theme on background paper. Stamped images can be coloured, cut out and used like stickers to lend an accent colour or design to a layout. Choose inks in colours that complement the layout, or scribble a felt-tip pen over a stamp, spray lightly with water, then press down. Alphabet stamps are useful for titles.

▼ *Collect postcards, currency and timetables as travel mementoes.*

Paint

Acrylic paint can be used to create any design on backing paper, and the huge range of colours available means you can match any shade in a photograph. Ready-mixed paint in tubes is easy to apply and very fine lines can be drawn using the nib.

Templates

All kinds of templates are available to help you customize layouts. They are an economical option since it's easy to create many different looks with just one template.

Fibres

Lengths of fibre add softness and texture to layouts, and provide contrast with the flatness and hard edges of card and paper. Luxurious knitting wool or ribbons can also be used. Mixed packs can be bought already colour co-ordinated. Try wrapping fibres round the bottom of a photograph, or threading a handful through a tag.

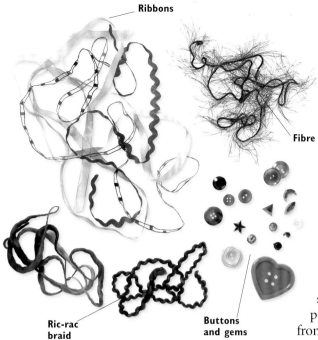

Ribbons

Fibre

Ric-rac braid

Buttons and gems

▲ *Fibres, braids and buttons can be used as borders for pictures or to hold items in place.*

Buttons and gems

Stitch or stick these to a layout as embellishments, or to anchor journaling blocks. You could use a gem to dot the "i" in a title, or scatter several in the corner of a photograph. Delicate pearl buttons are especially suited to baby themes or heritage layouts.

Memorabilia

Real or replica memorabilia adds significance to a layout. When you go travelling, for example, save ephemera such as tickets, timetables and restaurant bills to combine with your photographs. Failing the real thing, you can buy a replica pack. Foreign stamps, used or unused, and paper currency are other authentic additions.

Memorabilia pockets

Tuck small items of memorabilia in pockets to keep them safe but accessible. Pockets that have clear fronts allow you to see what's inside without taking it out.

Attachments

There are lots of specialist attachments available now, which can be kept as they are or further embellished by sanding, painting or stitching. Tuck a special souvenir in a pre-made pocket, or hang a key or zipper pull from a length of ribbon.

Metal

Embellishments sold for scrapbooks have been specially coated to prevent damage to layouts. Use brads or eyelets to fix vellum or tags in place. Thread ribbon or fibres through charms, or place a tiny key next to a heart. Photo turns are attached with brads and can hold hidden journaling closed but accessible. For quick attachment of ribbons, use coloured staples.

Adhesive mesh

This is available in strips or sheets and quickly adds texture to a layout. Dab ink or chalk over the surface then peel off, to give a shadowed texture pattern on paper.

Slide mounts

Cover these in paper or paint, then use as tiny picture frames or to highlight part of a photograph.

Paper charms

Embossed printed and foiled charms can be cut out and added to layouts.

▼ *Paper charms.*

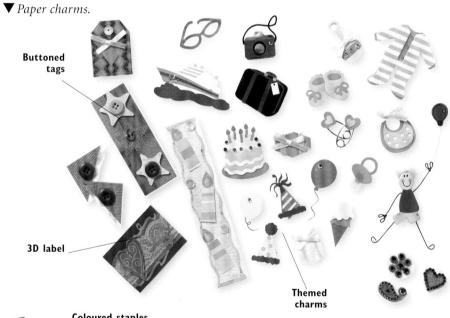

Buttoned tags

3D label

Themed charms

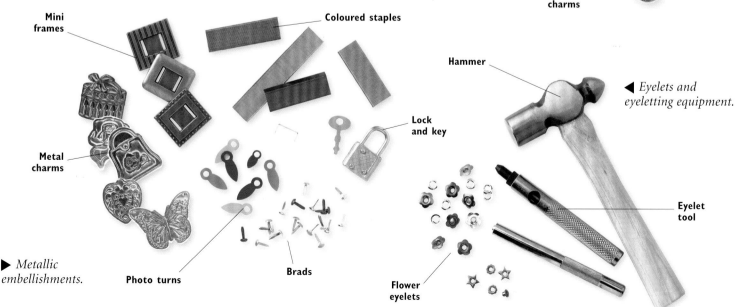

Mini frames

Coloured staples

Metal charms

Lock and key

Hammer

◄ *Eyelets and eyeletting equipment.*

Eyelet tool

▶ *Metallic embellishments.*

Photo turns

Brads

Flower eyelets

Lettering

The words you add to your layouts add an all-important dimension. Use the title to establish the theme of the page, bringing out the character of the layout in your treatment of the main word or perhaps an illuminated initial.

Letter templates

Use these in reverse to trace individual letters on to the back of your chosen paper, then flip over, to avoid having to erase pencil lines. Or use right side up to trace a title directly on to a layout, then colour with pencils or pens.

Letter stickers

The quickest and easiest way to add titles to your pages is with adhesive stickers. Align the bases of the letters along a ruler or use a special plastic guide for curved lines of lettering. Mix colours and styles for a fun approach. Letter squares can be used in both positive and negative forms, making them versatile and economical. Tweezers or a crocodile clip are useful in helping to place letter stickers accurately.

Cut-out letters

These are available in sheets or as part of themed paper collections, and make good decorative initials. Cut them out individually and glue down, or mount on foam pads for added dimension. A large number of styles are available to suit any scrapbook theme.

Buttons

Some manufacturers offer sets of letters in a range of different formats, such as small buttons. You could glue or stitch them on to a layout, or thread a name on thin ribbon and drape it over a photograph. Use a single button for the initial letter of a word to highlight it.

▼ *Lettering stickers and tools.*

SPECIAL PENS

These useful tools for correcting, labelling and safeguarding pictures are available from scrapbooking stores and craft suppliers.

Photo labelling pencil

This is a soft pencil for making notes on the back of photographs. Use black or white, depending on the colour of the paper on the back of the photograph, and press very lightly.

Acid-testing pen

Use one of these to test the pH level of light-coloured paper or ephemera. Draw a line and watch the ink change colour then check it against the scale printed on the side of the pen. It is a useful tool to test whether products you already have will be suitable for scrapbooking.

Red-eye reduction pen

Dot this gently over the red eyes in an otherwise successful photograph, and the green ink will balance out the red colour. A special version for pets' eyes is also available.

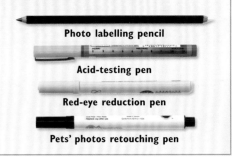

Photo labelling pencil

Acid-testing pen

Red-eye reduction pen

Pets' photos retouching pen

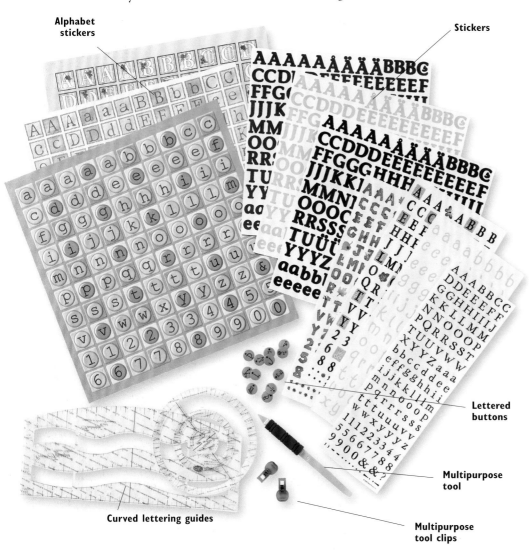

Alphabet stickers

Stickers

Lettered buttons

Multipurpose tool

Curved lettering guides

Multipurpose tool clips

▲ *Use lettering templates to trace individual letters for titles, then fill in with ink or pens or cut out and glue in place on the page.*

Tools for journaling

While titles and captions can identify the people in the pictures, journaling goes further, explaining the background to an event and capturing its mood. Writing by hand adds a personal touch.

▶ *Fibre-tipped pens are easy to use and available in a wide range of colours and widths.*

Plain lettering

Wedding template

Decorative lettering

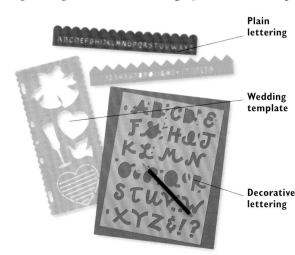

▲ *Plastic templates and stencils are available in a wide range of different styles of lettering and themes.*

◀ *Printed journaling blocks can be filled in by hand and then glued on to the album page.*

Templates
Scrapbooking templates in decorative shapes can be used to help you fit and align journaling. Trace one of the shapes on to the page and draw in guidelines with a soft pencil. Rub out the lines when the text is complete. Alternatively, draw round the shape and cut it out of contrasting paper. Add the journaling, erase the guidelines, then glue the paper shape on the layout.

Writing guide
Rest this on the paper and rest your pen lightly on the top of the wire loops as you write. The flexible loops will bend out of the way for the tails of letters descending below the level of the line.

Pens
Fibre-tip pens give good, even coverage. Use the tip for fine writing, and the side to create striking titles.

Fine-tipped pens
Use these when a lot of information has to be written in a small space, as their fine point allows for very neat writing. Fine tips can also be used to decorate titles drawn with thicker pens.

Gel pens
Manufactured in a wide range of colours, gel pens are a scrapbooker's staple. Metallic shades look good on dark paper.

Paint pens
These draw a wide, opaque line of colour, perfect for large titles or for outlining photographs instead of matting.

Computer fonts
A computer will give you access to an almost limitless range of fonts and sizes available for titles and journaling. Titles can be printed out and mounted on a layout, but for a more striking effect, print a title in reverse and cut it out, then flip it over and add to the page. Printing in reverse means any lines will not be seen on the finished layout.

Printed journaling boxes
Sets of journaling boxes offer pre-made titles and sayings to add to a layout, along with some blanks for you to record personal information. These are often produced to coordinate with paper sets, making it easy to complete a layout.

▶ *Fibre-tipped and gel pens are suitable for titles and journaling.*

Flexible nylon loops

▲ *A writing guide keeps your handwriting horizontal when journaling without obstructing the movement of the pen.*

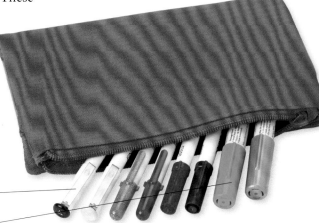

Fine-tipped pens

Round-tipped pens

CREATIVE IMAGE-MAKING

Whether you're sorting through boxes of old family pictures or taking new ones with your album in mind, these ideas will help you develop your visual sense and explore imaginative ways of using photographs to create some really arresting images.

Taking good photographs

The craft of scrapbooking sprang from a desire to present photographs of family and friends in a creative and meaningful way, and good photographs are the heart of every album page. So here are some tips to help you take more effective pictures for really stunning layouts. Modern cameras, equipped with high-quality lenses, built-in automatic exposure meters and sophisticated auto-focusing systems, can do nearly all the work for you. Unless you choose to manage your camera's settings manually for creative effects, you really can just point and shoot terrific pictures. However, technical quality is meaningless if your pictures are badly composed, coarsely lit or just lifeless.

Whether you're using a state-of-the-art SLR or a disposable camera, you need to train your eye to make the most of light, colour and form, and learn how to see your subject as the camera sees it to achieve the effective results you want.

Even if you are a good photographer, you are bound to have some pictures that don't come out right, with too much background or foreground, subjects disappearing off the edge of the photo or, if you've used flash, people with red eyes. All is not lost: there are ways of improving many pictures that will enable you to display them.

Photographing people

Whether they're formally posed or candid shots, photographs of people should aim to convey their true character. Most people feel ill-at-ease or put on some kind of show when you first point a lens at them, so it's best to take lots of pictures. Children, especially, will soon forget about the camera's presence if they're busy playing, leaving you to get your best photographs.

For candid shots, a telephoto or zoom lens means your subjects need not be aware of the camera at all. It will also throw the foreground and background out of focus, adding emphasis to the subject, which is just what you want.

Lighting

The traditional instruction to "shoot with the sun behind you" when taking pictures outdoors tends to produce the flattest effect. If your subject is a person looking at the camera, this position will leave them squinting uncomfortably. It can be much more effective to move them into the shade of a tree or a building, where the indirect light will be much more flattering and the contrasts less extreme, making it possible to capture every detail.

If you are taking pictures in direct light, it's best to move yourself or your subject so that the light is coming from one side. This is easiest to achieve when the sun is low in the sky – early in the morning or in the late afternoon (which photographers call the "magic hour"). Indoors, a similar atmospheric sidelight can be provided by daylight coming through a window, which is wonderful for portraits.

Composing pictures

As you look through the viewfinder, or at the LCD screen of a digital camera, it's easy to concentrate too hard on the main subject of your picture, but it's important to see how the whole picture works within the frame. Before you focus and shoot, move the camera around to find the best angle. If necessary, change your position entirely to get a better angle, or to bring in some foreground interest.

Think about the background too: try to find an angle that gives a background that's attractive but not distracting, and look out for ugly details like power lines. If anyone appears to have a tree growing out of their head, move slightly to one side to avoid the problem.

▼ *Here the photographer has successfully used the rule of thirds to make a visually interesting image, but has tilted the camera so that the horizon is not level.*

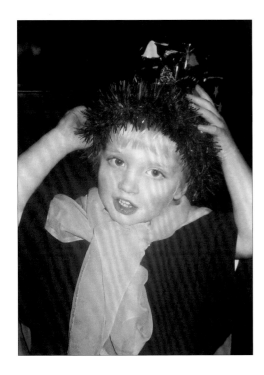

If you're photographing people, move in as close as you can to fill the frame. Alternatively, use a zoom lens – this also has the advantage of flattening the perspective, which has a flattering effect. With children, crouch or kneel to get yourself down to their level.

Try turning the camera on its side. A vertical, or "portrait", format is often better for pictures of people, but that's not always the case. If you're taking the photograph in an interesting setting,

▼*If you forget to check what's going on in the background of a picture while focusing on smiling faces, you can end up with an object appearing to grow out of someone's head.*

◀▲ *Red eyes appear when a subject is looking directly at the camera when the flash goes off. The problem is easy to rectify with a red-eye pen. Use it like a felt-tipped pen to mask out the unwanted red tones.*

including more of the the surroundings in a "landscape" format may convey more information about your subject. For example, you might portray a keen gardener in the context of the garden that they have created.

The most interesting pictures rarely have the main subject right in the centre. Photographers tend to follow the "rule of thirds", which involves visualizing a grid dividing the picture vertically and horizontally into three. Placing your subject on one of the four points where the imaginary lines intersect gives a harmonious composition.

Cropping prints

If you have a photograph where the main focus is too far off to one side, or the subject is set against a busy, distracting background, it is easy to crop the picture to eliminate the unnecessary parts and balance up the composition.

Rather than cutting off the unwanted part of the picture by eye and ending up with a lopsided picture, cut out two L-shaped pieces of black card (card stock). You can use these to form a rectangular frame of any size so that you can judge the part of the picture you want to use. Adjust the L-shapes backwards and forwards until you find the crop that looks best, then mark the print with a pencil. Cut along the marked lines using a craft knife and metal ruler and working on a cutting mat. Cropping pictures will give you a variety of different-sized prints, which can often add interest to album pages. You can

even remedy pictures that are crooked by cropping a little: draw a new frame parallel with the horizon in the photograph and trim all the edges to produce a straight image.

Red eyes

If people are looking straight at the camera when you take pictures using flash, the light reflects on their retinas, causing their eyes to shine red. Professional photographers use lights set at a distance from the camera to avoid this problem, and some compact cameras that rely on inbuilt flash have a "red-eye reduction" setting, which can help. Another solution is to take pictures when your subjects are not looking directly into the lens.

If you do want to use photographs in which people looking directly at the camera have red eyes, you can improve your prints using a red-eye pen, available from photograhic suppliers. This is a dark green marker pen that successfully counteracts the red, leaving the eyes looking dark. Simply colour in all the red eyes visible on the photograph, taking care not to mark the rest of the faces. The ink is permanent so the colour will not smudge, and your pictures will look much better.

▲ *Everyone has the odd print like this in their collection: most of the sky can simply be cropped away to focus on the main subject.*

▶ *Many badly framed pictures can be redeemed by judicious cropping, but try out your ideas with an adjustable frame, easily made from two pieces of black card, before you start cutting up a print.*

Tinting photographs

Black-and-white photographs, particularly those that have not faded with age, can sometimes look stark in a photograph album. One way to enliven them and give them more interest is to tint them with coloured inks.

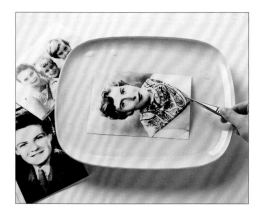

1 Select the photographs to be hand-tinted. Pour some water mixed with the ink thinner solution into a shallow tray. Using a pair of tweezers, add one photograph at a time to the solution.

2 Place the wet photo on a board and wipe the excess water from it using a cloth. The photo should be damp rather than wet, or the ink will run where the water is rather than where you want it to go.

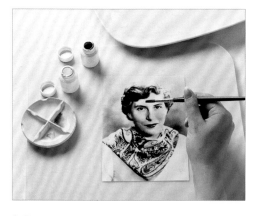

3 Pour a little thinner solution into a palette and add a drop of ink. Apply the colour gently using a fine paintbrush and wait for it to be dispersed by the damp print before adding more. Test the colours to see how different they appear once dry.

4 Add touches of colour to the hair, eyes and lips. Darken the colour as necessary to suit the person in the photograph. Finally, add a few touches of colour to the clothing. Leave the photograph to dry thoroughly before mounting it.

COLOURING MEDIA

Oil-based inks specially formulated for colouring photographs are available in a range of colours and are sold with a thinner solution that can be used to prepare the surface of the print and to dilute the colour. Special marker pens are also available, and can be easier to use for small areas of colour, though the use of a brush can give a more authentic period look. You could also experiment with other media, such as coloured pencils.

The degree to which the colour "takes" will depend on the type of paper used to make the print: if possible select matt prints for colouring as the surface has more grip and will hold the ink more successfully than gloss.

Traditionally, when all photography was in black and white, the most common use for hand-colouring was to add flesh tones to portraits, and doing this will give your prints a period feel. When painting faces, however, take care not to overdo the inking, or your pictures will end up looking like caricatures. If you add too much colour to start with it cannot easily be removed. Use very dilute inks and test all the colours first on a copy of the photograph to ensure that you are happy with the effect and so that you do not risk ruining the original print.

VIRTUAL HAND-TINTING

If you have image-editing software, such as Adobe Photoshop, on your computer, you can apply all kinds of colour effects before making prints. In the example shown here the colourful background was felt to be too dominant and has been selectively converted to black and white so that the album pages stand out more strongly. If you wish to "age" existing black-and-white prints digitally you can scan the images into the computer and add effects such as sepia toning, vignetting or hand-tinting, then print new copies.

Making a photographic mosaic

Try this simple technique to give added interest to an image with bold shapes and colours, or to create an overall pattern from a more detailed picture. Simply cut the print up into a series of small squares and then reassemble it on a coloured background, leaving narrow spaces between the shapes. Mosaic works best on more abstract subjects, or shots of the natural world like these two flower pictures. If you are working with pictures of people, don't make any cuts through the faces as this will alter their proportions.

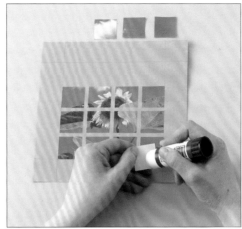

1 Working on a cutting mat, use a clear ruler and a sharp knife to cut the picture into strips of equal width, 2.5–3cm/1–1¼in wide. Cut each strip into squares, keeping them in the correct order as you work to avoid ending up with a jigsaw. A 10 × 15cm/4 × 6in print can be divided into 24 squares each measuring 2.5cm/1in; larger prints can be cut into more squares, or larger squares, as desired.

2 Decide how much space you want around the completed mosaic and how wide to make the distance between the squares. Lightly rule a border on to your chosen backing paper. Starting at the bottom left corner, stick down the first row of squares, making sure that the gaps between them are regular. Continue working upwards until you reach the end of the last row.

3 For a less structured approach, try using a punch to cut out the squares. This method leaves larger, irregular spaces between the picture elements and the finished look resembles a traditional mosaic made from tesserae. Adhesive foam pads add an extra dimension to the finished image. Make sure you are going to punch out a complete square by opening the little flap underneath the cutter and inserting the photograph face down in the punch.

NOW TRY THIS

These two mosaics show complementary variations on the technique. A photograph of russet, gold and green branches takes on an abstract feel when divided into squares, while a picture of rich autumnal foliage provides the perfect frame for a study of a noble tree.

Making a photographic patchwork

Traditional patchwork blocks have a strong geometry, which provides a ready-made framework for floral photographs. Designs such as the hexagonal "Grandmother's Flower Garden" are ideal for showing off your favourite garden pictures, and flowers such as primulas, pansies and apple blossom are reminiscent of the pretty prints on old-fashioned dressmaking fabrics. Look for formal carpet bedding, fields of colourful crops or wild flowers, and take both wide-angle and close-up photographs of them to use in creating your own interpretations of these patterns.

NOW TRY THIS

This bright chequerboard is made up of alternate squares: one a close-up of a poppy flower, the other a wider shot of the field in which it grew. Both pictures were given a pop art look by digitally increasing the contrast and brightness of the original images. The squares butt up to each other so that no background shows through.

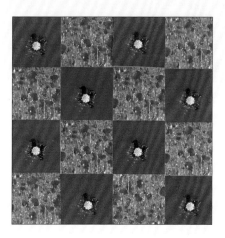

I Use a patchwork template to cut out a series of hexagons from your prints – you will need to make several copies of each photograph. The centre of each motif is cut from a single close-up and the six hexagons that surround it are made from pictures of massed flowers in a bed.

2 Take time to arrange the shapes before sticking them down, making sure that you have enough of each type. Starting at the bottom left corner, glue six patterned hexagons around a plain coloured one. Leaving a 6mm/¼in space all around, make more interlocking motifs to fill the page. Trim the edges flush with the background.

Weaving photographic images

This technique requires planning, but the results are well worth it and often produce unexpected effects. Experiment by combining a black-and-white and a coloured copy of the same photograph to create extra depth, as shown with the picture of a Japanese news stand, or by weaving an abstract photograph of texture with a landscape. Weaving works best on landscape or abstract images: as with photographic mosaics, avoid using close-up portraits.

I For a square weave, cut the black-and-white version of the picture into horizontal strips 2cm/³⁄₄in wide, stopping just short of one end so that they remain joined together. Use a sharp knife and a transparent ruler, and work carefully on a cutting mat. Cut the coloured picture into separate vertical strips of the same width.

2 Weave the first strip from the left of the coloured picture under and over the black-and-white strips. Take the second strip and weave it under the alternate strips: repeat this to the end, making sure that they are all at right angles and that the space between them is minimal. Secure the ends of the strips with double-sided tape and display the finished piece in a window mount.

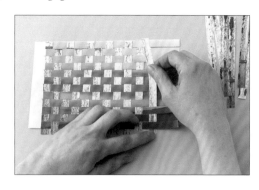

3 To create a basket weave, in which the horizontal strips form rectangles and the vertical ones squares, leave a 3mm/⅛in gap between the short strips. Two very different pictures – one of a stunning coastal sunset and the other of a rusting iron shed – are combined in this weave. They work well together because they have very similar colour schemes.

Making panoramas and compositions

Panoramic cameras are fun to use but you don't actually need one to make your own panorama. If you take two or more photographs from the same viewpoint, turning the camera slightly each time, you can then trim and stick the photographs together to make a long, narrow view. You can also use variations on this technique to create extended panoramas from just a single image or use your imagination to combine different images, with surprising results.

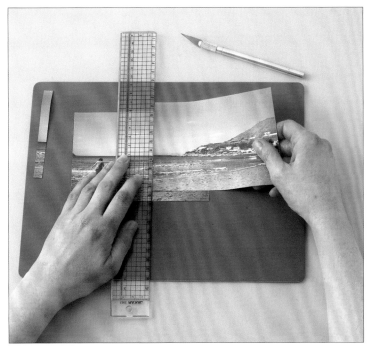

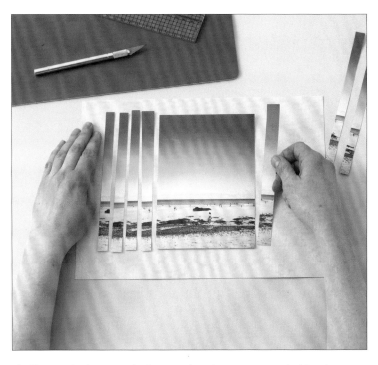

▲ If you are making a joined panorama remember that photographs tend be slightly darker towards the edges (a natural consequence of producing a rectangular image with a round lens) so it's best not to butt untrimmed vertical edges together. Instead, overlap the pictures to see how much of the image they share, then trim half this width from one picture. Put them together with the trimmed photo on top, align a ruler with the trimmed edge, slide away the top picture and trim the bottom one.

▲ Turn a single portrait-format view into an extended landscape, or composite panorama, by combining two identical prints. Cut strips of varying width from each side of one photograph and mount them either side of your main image. If you leave narrow spaces between them, it is less obvious that they simply repeat the image rather than extending it.

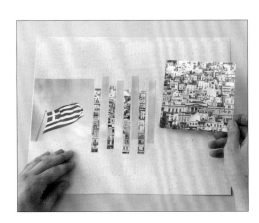

▲ An interesting variation on the composite panorama is to use two very different but related pictures to encapsulate memories of an event or place. Here a photograph of a Greek flag is interspersed with a geometric abstract view of buildings clinging to the steep hillside of the Cycladic island of Syros. Staggering the strips adds to the geometric nature of the images.

▲ A quick way to join two similar pictures is to find an obvious vertical line or strong outline along the edge of one of them and cut along it. You can then overlay this edge across the other picture. Although the two pictures used here were not taken from the same spot, they share the same colours and tonal range, so give the effect of two people appearing in the same photograph.

▲ *A great way to produce a multifaceted image of an event or scene is as a photo-composite, in the style of artist David Hockney. To do this, take lots of pictures from different angles and combine them in a collage. This view of the lake and Palm House at the Royal Botanic Gardens in Kew, London, includes several photographs of the same pair of swans, creating the illusion of a larger flock.*

Transferring photographs on to fabric

Several types of special paper are available for transferring photographs on to fabric. Your pictures will not be damaged by the process but it must be undertaken at a photocopy bureau. Copy several photographs together on to one sheet. Make sure you have enough transfers to allow for experimentation and mistakes. Some photographs do not work well on transfer paper, such as those with dark backgrounds or lots of contrast, so be prepared for some trial and error.

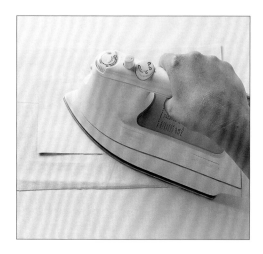

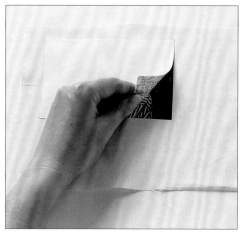

1 Stick the photographs lightly on to a piece of plain paper. Take this to a colour copy bureau together with the transfer paper, which needs to be fed one sheet at a time through the paper tray. (Have the photographs copied using a normal colour process to check the colour before they are copied on to the transfer paper.) Trim around a transfer and place it face down on a plain natural fabric with a close weave, such as calico, which will withstand heat and pressure. Referring to the manufacturer's instructions, press with a hot iron. If a lot of pressure is required, it may be advisable to work on a sturdy table protected with several layers of blanket.

2 Carefully peel off the transfer backing in an even movement to reveal the transferred image. Allow the fabric to cool before using it. Refer to the transfer paper manufacturer's instructions for washing and aftercare. A more expensive, but generally foolproof method of photo transfer is to have the process done professionally at a copy bureau that prints T-shirts with your own images.

NOW TRY THIS

This endearing photograph of a much-loved pet required special treatment. The image was transferred on to a piece of natural linen and the vintage-style fabric that forms the frame was carefully selected to echo the paisley quilt the kitten is sitting on. A narrow lace edging and pearl buttons complete the frame.

NOW TRY THIS

This sophisticated cloth book would make a wonderful keepsake for a young child. Take close-up photographs of familiar scenes around the child's house and garden and transfer them on to a coarsely woven fabric such as linen or calico to give them a canvas-like texture. Trim each one to 12.5cm/5in square and tack (baste) it to a 16.5 x 18cm/6¹/₂ x 7in felt rectangle, allowing a 2cm/³/₄in border around three sides and a wider border at the spine. Attach with a decorative machine stitch, then assemble the pages and stitch along the spine. You could also embellish the pages with embroidered messages, printed text or other appliquéd decoration.

Making a kaleidoscope

The multi-faceted image inside a kaleidoscope is created by reflecting an image between two angled mirrors to produce a repeating, symmetrical pattern. With patience it is possible to make your own photographic version: the effect is stunning, complex, and can be slightly surreal, as with this reinterpretation of a Venetian canal scene. You will need eight prints of the same picture, four of them reversed.

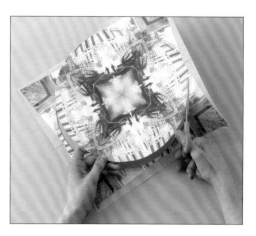

1 Draw a square on acetate or tracing paper and divide it diagonally to make a triangular template. Cut it out and use to make two sets of four triangles from the photographs. Clear acetate will enable you to position the template accurately so that the images are identical, with one set a mirror image of the other.

2 Mark a square sheet of paper into eight equal sections: these will be your guidelines for assembling the pattern. Matching the sides of the images exactly, glue the segments in place, making sure that each one lies next to its mirror image.

3 You can then trim the finished pattern as you wish: into a square, a four-point star or, as here, a circle. Mark the circumference with a pair of compasses and cut around the pencil line.

4 If you choose an image that is already symmetrical you can make a kaleidoscope from four, six or eight prints without having to reverse them. Here, the iconic image of the Eiffel Tower is surrounded by pictures of a period shop front to create a unique souvenir of Paris.

NOW TRY THIS

Here, eight diamonds form the design known in patchwork as the LeMoyne Star, giving the original flower image an abstract quality.

Framing and mounting photographs

There are many possible ways to frame your favourite photographs and cards. All the ideas shown here are quick and easy to do and look very effective, both in album pages and as fresh ways of displaying photographs in frames. Try them on your own layouts, or use them as inspiration for your original ideas.

CUTTING PAPER FRAMES

Single or multiple borders in paper or thin card (stock), known as mats, are a simple way to present a picture, but must be accurately cut for successful results. Choose colours that match or contrast effectively with the dominant colours in the photographs, and make sure that each successive border balances the photograph and is evenly positioned around the picture.

▲ *On this album page attention is focused on a single image by mounting it in a double mat in two colours. The opening in the top layer is cut a little larger to expose a narrow contrasting inner border.*

▲ *In this charming treatment the paper border is arranged some way away from the edge of the photograph, so that the background acts as an inner frame. A spray of die-cut daisies completes the effect.*

▲ *Multiple paper frames in a simple colour scheme are a great way to give unity to a diverse collection of photographs and other memorabilia. Extra layers can be added to disguise differences of size.*

▼ *For this stacked technique the subject is cut out first and used as the template for the border shapes, each drawn 6mm/¹⁄₄in larger than the layer above. The careful choice of graduated tones, complementing the bird's plumage, gives a subtle three-dimensional effect.*

▲ *Here the background colour matches the vehicle, and contrast is provided by the square black frames, each of which has a window a little larger than the cut-out photograph, leaving a striking band of colour around each picture.*

USING TEMPLATES

Plastic templates are available in a host of different shapes and sizes, from simple geometric forms to outlines of cats and Christmas trees. You can also draw and cut your own from many sources. Basic shapes such as ovals are useful guides for trimming photographs accurately, and are easy to use.

1 Position a template over the part of the photograph you want to use and draw around the outline with a pencil.

2 Use a small, sharp pair of scissors to cut carefully around the pencil line.

▲ *Use a set of templates in graduated sizes to cut a series of mats or frames to fit around your picture.*

1 Cut out a narrow frame from a photograph with a lot of background to draw attention to the focal point.

2 Turn the cut-out section by 45 degrees and replace it between the central area and the border to complete the frame.

▲ *Alternatively, cut away the outer sections of the picture in regular shapes, then offset them slightly and glue to a backing sheet.*

▲ *For a rainbow effect, use a template to cut a succession of circles, then offset them.*

▲ *Make a frame to suit your subject, like this porthole for an underwater theme.*

▲ *Different framing methods are unified here by consistent use of colour and shape.*

TEARING PAPER FRAMES

Torn paper shapes can add softness and a change of texture to your layouts, but it's a good idea to use the effect sparingly, as it can easily become too dominant. Combine it with neat, straight edges for contrast, or make a mosaic of lots of small-scale torn edges using different colours for a subtle collage.

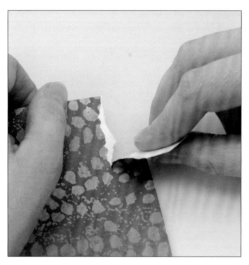

1 Tearing paper or card (stock) that is coloured the same shade all through gives a soft textured edge. The feathery lines are good for recreating textures such as teddy bear fur, or for layering to create backgrounds resembling water, clouds or grass. Tearing with the grain of the paper gives a straighter edge than tearing against the grain, so practise to see the effects you can achieve. To make it easier to tear a shape, try drawing with a dampened paintbrush along the line you want to tear.

2 Patterned paper is usually printed and has a white core. Tearing the paper will reveal this. Tearing towards yourself with the pattern uppermost produces a white edge, which highlights the tear. If you don't want to make a feature of this, tear the paper from the other side so that the rough white edge is concealed under the printed top layer. This is a good choice when you want to create a softer line, perhaps when overlapping torn edges to create a change of colour.

▲ *A sheet of torn mulberry paper in a toning colour makes a lovely textural border for a picture. Tearing this paper pulls out the fibres to make a softly fringed edge. The paper should be dampened where you want it to part. For a straight tear, fold it and wet the folded edge then gently pull it apart. For the more random tearing used here, dampen the paper by drawing curves and shapes with a wet paintbrush or cotton bud (swab).*

DECORATING PAPER FRAMES

You can use pre-printed stickers, but it is easy to make your own frames to suit a particular theme. Trace motifs from books or magazines on to plain paper and adjust the scale on a photocopier if necessary to make a template. Draw around or trace the design on to coloured paper and cut out as many shapes as you need, then glue them on to your album page.

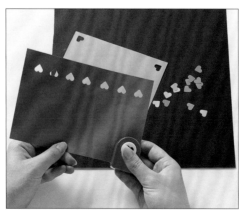

▲ *Specially shaped edging scissors are available in many different designs, and you can use these to create smart decorative effects on coloured paper frames.*

▲ *You can decorate the corners of frames with a punched motif, or punch rows of decorative holes all round the edge. Keep the shapes to decorate the rest of the album page.*

▲ *Use a template to cut decorative shapes from appropriately coloured paper to highlight the theme of an album page, and let them overlap the picture frames.*

▲ *Create an informal look by making a frame from printed stickers. Mount the photograph on a plain background then mass the stickers in groups around it, overlapping the edges and each other.*

▲ *A pricked design makes a pretty, lacy edging for a simple paper frame. Draw the design lightly in pencil then prick evenly along the lines with a bodkin, resting the frame on a soft surface such as a cork tile.*

▲ *Use a stamp of a frame and bright ink to make a frame on plain coloured paper. Cut out a wavy edge for a funky look.*

NOW TRY THIS

Instead of framing pictures, try mounting them over blocks of bright colour to create a collage effect, then frame them with groups of flowers in co-ordinating shades. These could be stickers or your own photographs, carefully cut out.

I Select individual flowerheads to match the colours in your pictures and cut them out, carefully eliminating any background.

2 Arrange the coloured paper shapes for the background and glue in place, then position the photographs.

3 Arrange the flower cut-outs to create a scattered effect over the background areas, co-ordinating the colours and allowing the petals to overlap the edges of the photographs.

BACKGROUND TREATMENTS

Rather than have plain backgrounds to the pages in your album, decorate them with stamps, stencils, stickers and paint effects in colours and themes that are sympathetic to your photographs. Choose subdued, muted shades for subtle compositions, or be more adventurous and experiment with unusual combinations of colour and pattern.

Choosing colours

The background should flatter the photographs rather than overpower them and its style needs to be in keeping with the subject matter. But you need not restrict your choice to a single colour or design: try making up collages of interesting textures and patterns. Include greetings cards, wrapping paper, children's artwork, and even fabric swatches.

COMPLEMENTARY COLOURS

1 Allow the photographs to dictate your choice of background colours, rather than choosing a paper and hoping the pictures will match it. Hold your images against a wide variety of colours and patterns before making your choice. Here the photograph is overpowered by the colour of the background paper.

▲ *Once you have decided on the images you want to mount, think about colours and motifs that underline their theme. These gold papers suit a wedding layout and the heart is a traditional symbol. Play around with combinations of papers until you find a good balance between images and background.*

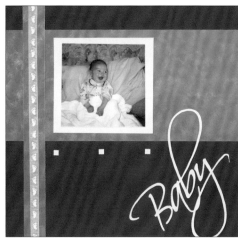

▲ *Blue is the traditional colour scheme for a baby boy, but the dark blue background overlaid with simple bands of lighter tones, with only tiny dashes of baby blue, give this simple treatment a modern look.*

2 Orange and green are opposite each other on the colour wheel, so they complement each other well and the cooler colour tends to recede, making the picture of the pumpkins stand out as the focal point. Against this background you could use accents of orange and other warm, toning colours such as peach and gold to accompany the image.

▲ *Do not shy away from patterned backgrounds; these scraps of delicately patterned wallpaper work beautifully with each other and the warm tones of the cat.*

▲ *If you place the same images on a different background, with colours that clash with the photographs, you can instantly see that it is an unsuitable combination.*

Using patterns

Patterned backgrounds help to give layouts a distinctive style, but need to be carefully chosen to avoid dominating the images and other elements that you may choose to add to the page. Make sure the colours and contrasts in the photographs are strong enough to stand out from the background.

MONOCHROME SCHEMES

An easy way to begin experimenting with pattern is to restrict your use of colour.

1 Gather together a selection of papers, patterned and plain, in a single colour. Experiment by overlapping them or placing them next to each other until you find an arrangement you like. Choose one as the background, and cut a few rectangles or strips from the other papers.

2 For this layout, cut a rectangle of plain blue paper 18 x 25cm/7 x 10in and a strip 5 x 30cm/2 x 12in from another pattern. Stick the rectangle to the left-hand side of the page, 2.5cm/1in in from the top, bottom and left side. Arrange the patterned strip horizontally across the page so it overlaps the lower part of the rectangle. Mat the photographs and add them to the layout.

▲ *Using the same design in a different colour scheme and with different subjects changes the look entirely. Here, the monochromatic green layout includes touches of pale yellow in the flower and buttons to pick up the yellow details in the photographs.*

COMBINING PATTERNED PAPERS

Many ranges of patterned paper are specially designed to be used in combination, making it easy to create interesting backgrounds.

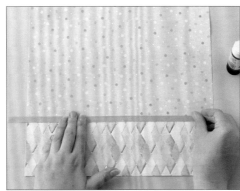

1 This design mimics a wall with wallpaper and a dado rail, the perfect place to display a few photos. Choose a 30cm/12in square sheet of paper for the background and cut a strip of another paper 10cm/4in wide.

2 Glue the strip to the bottom of the page and cover the join with a length of toning ribbon. Arrange two large photographs on the upper part of the page. With a button and an extra length of ribbon, suspend a smaller photo from the ribbon "rail".

▲ *These two papers harmonize perfectly because although the patterns contrast in shape and scale they are printed in the same range of colours. When mixing patterns, go for colours in the same tonal family and try teaming stripes with floral designs, or look for the same motifs in different sizes.*

USING STRIPES AS BORDERS

If you are combining striped and patterned paper, the stripes can be cut up to form a border around the page and frames for the photographs.

1 Choose a paper with wide stripes, and cut four identical strips 4 × 30cm/1¹/₂ × 12in. Mount one on each side of the page, matching the stripes. Glue another along the bottom and mitre the corners by cutting diagonally through both layers.

2 Add the last strip at the top of the page, making sure the strips correspond as before, and mitre the two top corners. Mat your selection of photographs in toning shades and mount on the page.

▲ *Four black-and-white photographs of disparate subjects are neatly unified with this simple treatment, which does not distract attention from the pictures.*

USING BOLD PATTERNS

Some patterned papers are bold and dramatic but won't overwhelm photographs if they are paired with strong images or colours. Close-ups of faces or objects work best.

1 Choose a patterned paper that includes as many of the colours in your choice of photographs as possible. Here the bright pinks and oranges pick up the colours of the flowers and the vivid stripes convey the exuberance of spring blossom.

2 Pick shades from the patterned paper to mat the photos: this will help them stand out from the background. Add embellishments that match the colour and theme of the layout.

▶ *The pretty ribbons on this page are chosen to match the striped paper, while the little flower buttons echo the springtime theme.*

Collage techniques

Building up a multilayered background using different papers allows you to introduce a satisfying variety of texture and colour.

USING MULBERRY PAPER

Mulberry paper is available plain or printed, and some sheets incorporate pieces of flowers or leaves, making perfect backgrounds for pictures with a pastoral or garden theme. Its soft feathered edges are very attractive.

I Choose a selection of papers that match the tones of the photograph. Strips of paper will be used to extend the bands of colour in the sky. To tear them, dip a paintbrush in water then trace a line on the paper. Pull the paper apart while it is wet.

2 Build up the scene with torn strips of mulberry paper; a different shade is created when two colours of the paper overlap. Mat the photograph in black, so that its straight edges form a striking contrast with the soft outlines of the mulberry paper, and mount it on the background.

▲ *This lovely photograph of a sunset has an almost abstract quality, and the collage background made with torn strips of mulberry paper extends the scene very effectively. The dark foreground, reduced to a silhouette in the fading light, is matched by a sheet of black paper covering the lower part of the page.*

MAKING A PAPER COLLAGE

Subtle colour effects can be achieved by building up small pieces of torn paper in a range of toning colours. Begin by tearing a good quantity of the colours you need before applying any glue.

I Tear the paper into small pieces of a fairly even size, aiming to make rounded shapes. Tear away the straight edges of the paper so that they are roughly torn on all sides.

2 Glue the pieces to the background in a group, overlapping them and mixing the colours at random. If you want to create the effect of falling leaves, you could add a scattering of isolated pieces.

3 Add details to the collage if you wish by stamping motifs or drawing them in with a fibre-tipped pen in a toning colour.

▶ *Here a photograph is enhanced by a colour-co-ordinated collage in subdued colours that has been aged with stamping.*

USING COLLAGED PAPER

Some patterned papers have a collage-effect design, with elements scattered across the paper. If you cut around parts of these, you can slide photographs underneath to look as if they are part of the overall design.

1 Mark with a pencil where a corner or edge of the photograph intersects with an element in the pattern. Use a craft knife to trim along the edge of the pattern.

2 Make more slits across the page to accommodate the photographs you wish to include. Mat the photos and slide them under the flaps.

▲ *Single elements, such as the suitcase on this travel-themed layout, can be trimmed from another sheet of patterned paper and added as embellishments.*

COLOUR BLOCKING

This is an easy technique to master, especially for beginners and when using a monochromatic colour scheme. Photographs and other elements can sit neatly within one block or overlap across several. This design for a 30cm/12in album page is based on a grid of 8 x 8 squares.

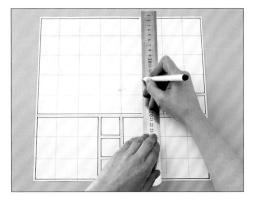

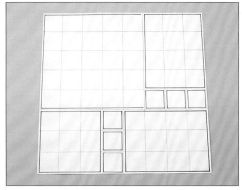

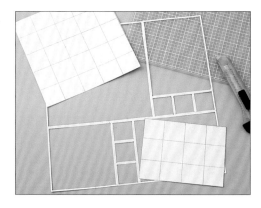

1 Using a grid of 4cm/1½in squares, design the blocks for your layout.

2 Rule 6mm/¼in margins between the blocks and all round the edge of the sheet.

3 Use a craft knife and ruler to cut each template piece out of the grid.

4 Draw round each template on the back of patterned paper and cut out. Use a different paper for each section.

5 Glue the cut-out papers on to a background sheet of 30cm/12in card (stock), following the original layout.

6 Add photographs, embellishments and journaling as desired.

Traditional patchwork patterns include lots of designs that can be adapted to scrapbooking. This one is called "Shoo Fly" and is a simple combination of squares and triangles in a balanced design to which photographs can be added.

1 Choose one 30cm/12in square paper for the background. From a different paper, cut three 10cm/4in squares. Cut two of these in half diagonally.

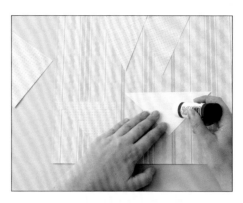

2 Position the background square centrally on the page, and arrange one triangle diagonally across each corner. Glue in place.

3 Add lines of "stitching" around the patches with a black pen to mimic running stitch and blanket stitch. Glue the remaining square in the centre.

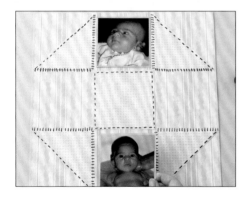

4 Arrange the photographs and embellishments between the patches.

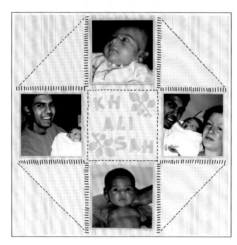

◀ *The patchwork theme is enhanced with drawn-in stitching and lettering designed to resemble appliqué.*

MAKING A SILHOUETTE

This makes an interesting treatment for a photograph of someone in profile. Cut the profile out of black or coloured card (card stock) to form an accompaniment to the photo. You can use the photograph as your guide for the silhouette, or you could draw your own version.

1 Using a computer or photocopier, enlarge the photograph to the desired size for the silhouette and glue to a sheet of dark card.

2 Cut carefully around the outline of the person in the print using a pair of sharp-pointed scissors.

3 Reverse the silhouette and add it to the layout, positioning it to balance the original photograph.

Adding paint, chalk and ink

Instead of using printed paper, you can create your own unique patterns to form tailor-made backgrounds for your collections. If you don't feel confident about your painting and drawing skills, just choose from the host of ready-made stencils and stamps available, and work with colour-washed backgrounds.

PAINTING BACKGROUNDS

For interesting textural effects, make patterns in wet paint. You can try a variety of objects such as the blunt end of a paintbrush, a cocktail stick (toothpick) or a wooden skewer, drawing simple curls, spirals and stars. Or cut a comb from stiff cardboard and draw it through the paint.

1 Mix some acrylic paint with wallpaper paste to make a thick paste. With a wide brush, paint the surface of a sheet of heavy cartridge (construction) paper using even strokes in one direction. Use a comb to make patterns in the wet paint.

2 Draw the comb in two directions for a woven pattern, or use random strokes for bark-like effects. Allow the paper to dry completely. If it buckles, press the back with a cool iron, then leave it between heavy books to keep it flat.

ANTIQUING

Paper with an aged look can be useful for heritage layouts, either as a background, as part of a collage, or for titles and journaling.

1 To achieve an antique effect, brush a strong solution of tea over the surface of white paper. Allow to dry, then press with a cool iron if necessary to flatten. The paper can then be torn or cut up to use in a collage. You could also try singeing the edges to add to the effect.

RUBBER STAMPING

There are literally hundreds of rubber stamps available on the market nowadays, so you will always be able to find something to complement your album page designs. You could use small motifs for surface decoration, or large scale designs that form an all-over background pattern.

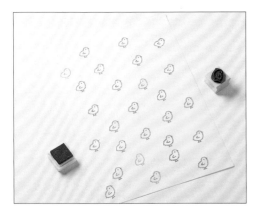

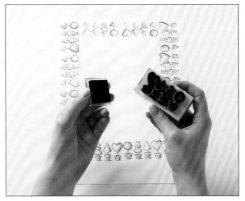

1 Use a single motif to stamp an all-over design on to plain paper to create a patterned background. Press the stamp in the ink pad, then press it on the paper, taking care not to smudge. Repeat as desired. Apply the images in a random pattern, or rule faint pencil guidelines.

2 The elongated shape of this topiary stamp makes it ideal for a border design. If you want a symmetrical design, measure the stamp and work out how many repeats will fit the page. Ensure the stamp aligns with the edge, and that each new print lines up with the designs already stamped.

3 Rubber-stamped designs can be enhanced very simply by colouring the motifs lightly with coloured pencils. You could also try using various kinds of paint to achieve different effects.

USING CHALKS

Sets of acid-free chalks are available in various ranges of different shades and can be used to create very soft colour effects on very light or very dark papers. To extend the tones of a photograph across a full layout, use chalks to recreate the scene, or use them to tint embossed paper.

1 Measure the photograph, subtract 1cm/⅜in from each side, and trace the dimensions on to a 30cm/12in square sheet of white card (stock). With a pad of cotton wool (ball), pick up some coloured chalk and rub it across the page.

2 Continue to build up the chalk scene, matching the shades used in the photograph and using a clean pad for each new colour. For details such as the path and fence posts, use a cotton bud (swab) or the applicator supplied with the chalk to draw finer lines.

3 Leave the page overnight, to allow the chalks to settle into the paper. Finally, add the photograph in the marked area.

COMBINING CHALKS AND STAMPING

Used together, rubber stamps and chalks enable you to combine fine pictorial detail with soft colouring. You can either use the chalks to fill in the stamped motifs or rub them over the paper to create a mist of colour over the whole page before applying the stamped image.

1 Choose rubber stamp motifs to match the theme of the page and stamp them at random over the background sheet using a range of coloured inks. Using a cotton wool pad (ball) rub chalks in toning colours across the page to create a soft wash of background colour. Leave the page for a few hours to allow the chalk to settle into the paper, then add the matted photographs and embellishments.

▶ *The smaller photograph of a leafy country track inspired the choice of leaf stamps in soft autumn shades for this background. The chalks harmonize well with the horse's colouring, and a length of real ribbon provides the finishing touch.*

STENCILLING

Charming backgrounds can be created using stencils, which work well with paints, oil sticks or chalks. Stencils are easy to cut from manila card or clear acetate, and you can work from templates or draw your own. Hundreds of ready-cut designs are also available in craft stores.

1 Trace the design and transfer it to stencil card. Working on a cutting mat and using a craft knife cut out each shape, taking care not to cut through any "bridges" holding elements of the design in place.

2 Using an oil stick or appropriate paint, and a large stencil brush, dab paint on to the chosen area using the stencil. Lift the stencil carefully to avoid smudging the edges and leave to dry.

3 Add details with a second stencil. Leave to dry.

▼ *Stencilled animals and a Noah's ark make a lovely setting for a young child's picture.*

EMBELLISHING THE PAGES

Adding the final decorative touches is often the most enjoyable part of assembling your album pages. The elements you use should enhance the photographs and complement the background.

Papercraft

Keep a collection of offcuts of interesting papers for these delicate decorations, which use precise folding and cutting to create pretty three-dimensional ornaments, from decorative tags and envelopes to classic origami flowers.

PAPER ROLLING

Rolled paper edgings and frames work particularly well when you use paper that is printed differently on each side, as the rolling exposes the contrasting pattern or colour.

▲ *The photographs here have been enhanced with rolled paper frames.*

1 To create a rolled heart, draw the shape on the back of the paper and cut a series of slashes from the centre to the edge.

2 Roll a dampened cotton bud (swab) along the cut edges to soften the fibres. Turn the paper over and roll each section towards the edge of the shape.

3 Glue a photograph or embellishment in the centre of the heart motif.

MAKING A LACÉ DESIGN

Pronounced "lassay", this technique works best when cut from two-sided card (stock). It can be cut using a metal template (you can buy lots of different designs) or you can devise your own using a pair of compasses or a protractor. Small patterned cuts are made in the card and the cut piece is bent over to form a bicoloured design.

1 Transfer the template to the wrong side of the card using a pencil (the lines will be erased later).

2 Using a sharp craft knife, cut neatly along the lines from end to middle. Erase the pencil marks and turn the card over.

3 Lift one petal and fold it backwards. Once all the petals are folded, tuck each one under the edge of the previous point.

PAPER APPLIQUÉ

Appliqué literally means "applied". Usually appliqué is a technique used with fabric in the art of patchwork. Here it is used with paper. Cut-out shapes in paper or card (stock) of different colours or patterns can be stacked together to create three-dimensional motifs. Here the appliqué effect is emphasized by lines of decorative "stitches" drawn around the card patches. Attaching the motif by means of sticky foam pads raises it a little above the surface, so that the butterfly seems to hover over the flowers.

1 Trace the outlines of the butterfly and the applied panels for the wings and copy them on to a sheet of card to make templates. Cut out all the pieces.

2 Select sheets of card in four different colours. Draw round the templates for the basic shape and the body in one colour, and divide the smaller coloured details between the remaining sheets, keeping the design symmetrical.

3 Cut out all the pieces of the butterfly.

4 Using a fine-tipped black pen, draw lines of small "stitches" around the edge of each coloured shape. Glue the shapes to the butterfly's wings. Create a pair of antennae from a length of fine silver wire, curling the ends tightly, and glue to the head. Attach the body to the wings using foam pads to give a three-dimensional effect, and use more foam pads to anchor the butterfly to the background.

▶ *This cut-out butterfly, floating a little above the surface of the album page, softens what would otherwise be a very rigid layout of squares, and is perfectly in keeping with the floral theme. The colours of the panels on its wings are repeated in the picture mats.*

QUILLING

Thin strips of finely rolled paper are arranged into pictorial images suitable for scrapbooking. This traditional craft requires a special tool and narrow strips of plain coloured paper, which you can buy specially cut. It is possible to cut them yourself but they must be precisely the same width all along their length. Once you've mastered your first roll (it's very easy) you can make this pretty flower.

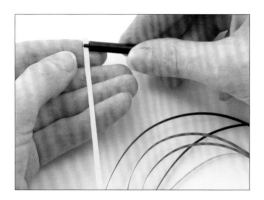

1 Make the leaves first. Slide one end of a green strip into the notch on the quilling tool.

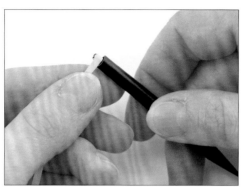

2 Roll the paper tightly and evenly on to the tool.

3 Gently ease the rolled paper off the tool and allow it to uncoil to the desired size. Glue the end and hold until dry.

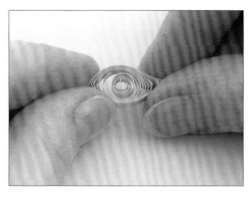

4 Pinch the edges of the circle on opposite sides, using your thumbs and forefingers.

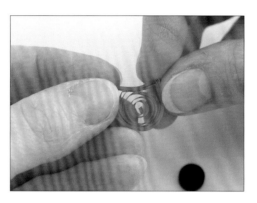

5 Make four red coils for the petals. Make two pinches close to each other, and press the rest of the circle down towards them.

6 Roll a tight black coil for the centre. Cut a stem from green paper and assemble the pieces to complete the poppy.

DECORATING TAGS

Tags are quick-to-make scrapbook embellishments and use only small quantities of materials. You can use a die-cutting machine or templates, or make the shape by just snipping the corners off a rectangle.

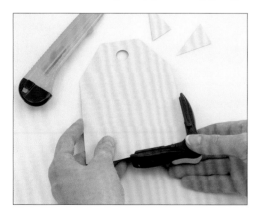

1 Snip two corners off a rectangle of card. Punch a hole for the string and shape the other two corners with a corner cutter.

2 Embellish the tag as desired. In this case ribbons and ribbon roses were used and the tag was tied with coloured fibres.

▲ *Use simple tags to hold pictures or text, or just as decoration. They can be glued to a page or hung by ribbon ties.*

MAKING POCKETS

As vellum is translucent, you can use this simple pocket for photos, or just slip some journaling or souvenirs such as tickets inside.

1 Cut out a pocket template and draw around it on vellum.

2 Fold in the side and bottom flaps. Glue the flaps and attach to the layout.

▼ *Vellum allows you to see what's inside the pocket without taking it out.*

MAKING MINI-ENVELOPES

A tiny envelope adds excitement to a page, and could be used to hold small treasures such as a handful of confetti in a wedding album, a scrap of lace or even a lock of hair. Or you could inscribe a secret message on a little card and tuck it inside.

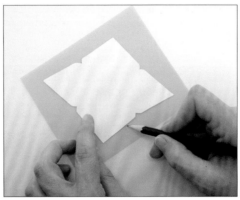

1 Draw around an envelope template and cut out.

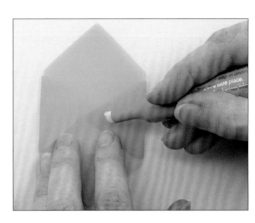

2 Fold in three of the corners and glue the overlapping edges. Fold down the top.

▶ *For a page celebrating the arrival of a baby girl, you could decorate some little envelopes with pretty labels and tiny pink bows.*

PLASTIC POCKETS

Cut a pocket from the lower edge of a stationery folder. Staple the sides together and insert a memento. Staple the top closed or leave it open so that the contents can be taken out.

Cut two squares from a plastic folder and pierce holes around the edges. Attach a memento or decorations to one piece using double-sided tape. Lace the sides together with cord and knot the ends.

MAKING POP-UP PAGES

Proper pop-ups like these party balloons work only on pages that aren't in page protectors, since it's the action of the pages opening out that makes the pop-up rise. You can, however, arrange lifting flaps on single pages inside page protectors, either by cutting a slit for them or by sticking them to the outside with another, cut-down, page protector to cover them. These pages are good for children's themes.

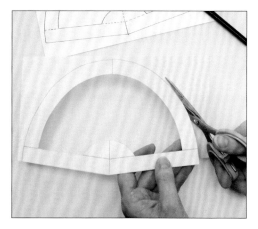

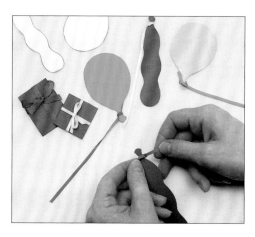

1 Transfer the pop-up template at the back of the book to white card (stock) and cut it out. Score along the dotted lines. Fold the bottom struts up and the arch back.

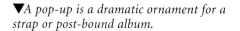

▼*A pop-up is a dramatic ornament for a strap or post-bound album.*

2 Apply adhesive to the bottom of the two struts, then glue the whole pop-up in place across two pages of the album. Following the templates, cut out the four balloons and two presents from plain card in a range of bright colours.

3 Wrap a ribbon round each present and tie ribbons round the ends of the balloons. Stick the parcels on the base of the pop-up, and balloons on the arch, making sure they will not jam the pop-up when it closes. Stick the tails of the balloons behind the parcels. Add photographs to the layout.

MAKING AN ORIGAMI SHIRT

This traditional craft of paper folding can be successfully exploited for scrapbooking designs. This clever little design really does look just like a tiny shirt, and makes a lovely embellishment for pictures of children playing at dressing up, or perhaps dressed for a special occasion. All the creases need to be sharp and accurate.

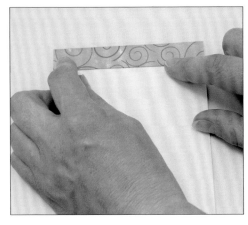

1 Cut a piece of patterned paper 10 × 20cm/4 × 8in. Fold in half lengthwise, then unfold. Fold down 1.5cm/½in from the narrow top edge. Fold over again.

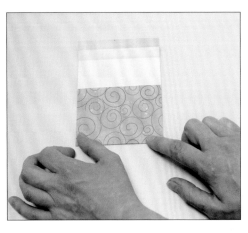

2 Unfold the two folds at the top, and fold up 7cm/2¾in from the bottom edge.

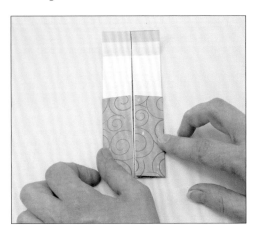

3 Fold the two long edges in to meet in the centre.

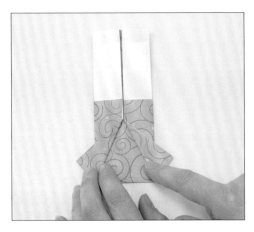

4 Fold out the bottom corners (these will form the sleeves).

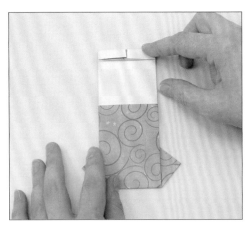

5 Turn over and fold the top edge down once, along the pre-existing crease.

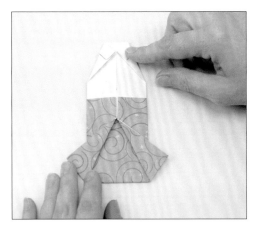

6 Turn over again and fold the top corners into the centre to form the collar.

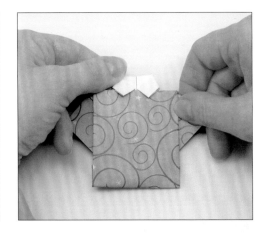

7 Fold in half horizontally, so that the original lower edge just touches the outer corners of the collar.

8 Tuck the points of the collar over the folded edge to complete the shirt. Add a bead necklace or a ribbon tie.

▲ For this page the shirt is neatly trimmed with a necklace threaded with a child's initial, and is accompanied by a little skirt made by concertina pleating a strip of paper in a toning colour. Photo mats using the two papers tie the whole scheme together.

TEA BAG FOLDING

This technique gets its unusual name because its inventor made her first fold using a colourful tea bag envelope. It's also known as miniature kaleidoscopic origami, and you can buy or download sheets printed with small patterned squares. The easiest design is a rosette, which can be used as a decorative element or as the "O" in a word like "snow" or "love".

1 Cut out eight patterned tea bag squares from a printed sheet.

2 Fold the first square diagonally, with the patterned side inside.

3 Unfold and turn the paper over so the back of the square is facing you.

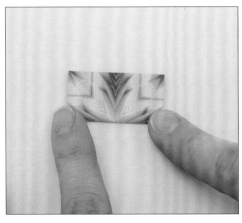

4 Fold the square in half horizontally, taking the bottom edge up to the top edge.

5 Unfold it, then fold it in half vertically, taking the right edge to the left edge with the patterned side inside. Unfold.

6 With the patterned side facing you, push the valley folds in and bring the two uncreased quarters of the square together.

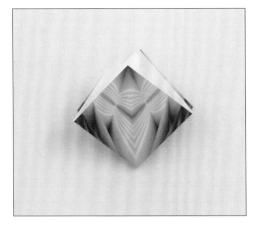

7 Fold all the remaining squares in the same way, then take one in your fingers, with the peak down and the open folds to the top.

8 Open the fold on one side, and spread some glue on it. Slide the next square, peak down, in between these two sticky sides, and press to make the glue stick.

9 Go round the circle, adding each square in the same way until the rosette is complete, then glue the last section over the first.

▲ *Adding green paper stems and simple leaf shapes to these tea bag rosettes turns them into stylized flowers to decorate a layout with a garden theme.*

10 Glue a cluster of beads or sequins in the centre to complete the decoration.

IRIS FOLDING

This technique creates intricate spiralling designs using folded strips of paper arranged like the panels of a camera iris. It is an ingenious method of creating curved forms using only straight components, and looks very effective when mounted inside an aperture. Experiment with combinations of plain and patterned paper or contrasting colours.

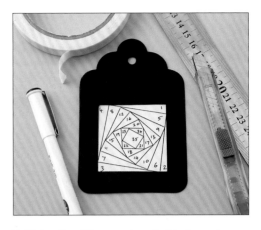

3 Cut a 5cm/2in aperture in black card (stock) and use low-tack masking tape to fix the template temporarily within the aperture. The pattern will be built up backwards, so place the black card face down on the table, with the template below.

1 Choose four different shades of paper and cut into strips 2cm/¾in wide.

2 Fold each strip in half lengthwise and glue the two sides together, right sides out.

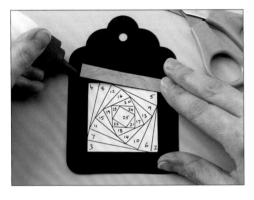

4 Cut a piece 6cm/2¼in long from a length of brown paper. Line it up to cover the triangle labelled 1, with the folded edge towards the centre. Glue the edges of the strip to stick it down (be careful not to get any adhesive on the template below).

5 Take a 6cm/2¼in length of pink paper, and glue it in position to cover the section marked 2 on the template.

6 Take a 6cm/2¼in length of blue paper, and glue it in position to cover the section marked 3 on the template.

7 Take a 6cm/2¼in length of green paper, and glue it in position to cover the section marked 4 on the template.

8 Continue round the spiral, adding paper strips as follows: brown (5), pink (6), blue (7), green (8), brown (9), pink (10), blue (11), green (12), brown (13), pink (14), blue (15), green (16), brown (17), pink (18), blue (19), green (20), brown (21), pink (22) blue (23), green (24).

9 The strips spiral into the centre, leaving a square hole (section 25 on the template).

▲ *This six-petalled flower design accentuates the spiralling shapes created in iris folding. This time just three different papers have been used, and a paper stem and leaves have been added to complete the picture.*

◄ *For this birthday page, three matching iris-folded squares have been turned into gifts with ribbon bows. The four papers used for the folds are repeated in the picture's frame.*

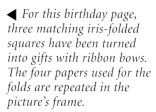

10 Cover the central hole by gluing on a square of brown paper.

11 Turn the card over and remove the template to reveal the completed design.

12 Turn the square into a house with a brown triangle for the roof and a folded paper chimney.

Adding metal and wire

Eyelets, wire decorations and metal tags add lustre and a change of texture to your layouts. Make sure hard materials of this kind are well protected and positioned so that they will not damage your precious photographs.

EMBOSSING METAL

Foil of around 38 gauge is suitable for embossing, working on the back to create a raised pattern, or on the front to indent a pattern.

1 To make a tag, draw round a card tag on a sheet of foil using an embossing tool or dry ballpoint pen and a ruler.

2 Cut out the tag with old scissors, trimming 2mm/¹⁄₈in outside the embossed line. Punch a hole in the top of the tag.

▲ *A simple outline of evenly spaced dots makes a pretty decoration for small metal picture frames.*

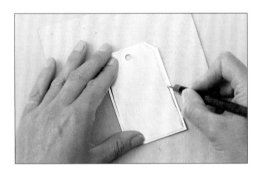

3 Place the tag face down on thick cardboard and emboss a row of dots inside the marked line. Add other motifs as desired and glue on a photograph or message.

◀ *For extra charm add some small motifs such as stylized flower shapes or these simple stars.*

USING WIRE

Fine wire in silver, gold and other colours can be twisted into delicate coils and curls and used in conjunction with paper decorations, fabric or ribbon flowers, sequins or clay ornaments.

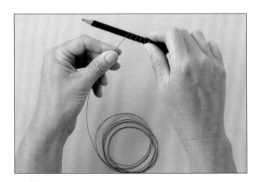

1 To make a coil, wrap some coloured wire around a pencil, then slide it off and trim.

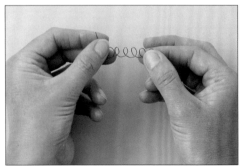

2 Flatten the coils with your fingers and glue the wire in place on the layout.

▲ *A wire coil makes an offbeat stem for a punched flower decoration in shiny plastic.*

INSERTING BRADS

Brads or paper fasteners are a decorative way to attach pictures.

1 To attach a picture to a tag, cut a small slit in each corner of the picture, and corresponding slits in the tag.

2 Push in the brads and open out the pins on the back, pressing them flat. Cover with small pieces of sticky tape if desired.

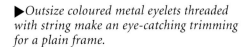

▲ *Brads can be used to hold layers of papers and embellishments together or they can be used for purely decorative purposes.*

▼ *This picture is held in place on its mount with eyelets in each corner, through which a length of fibre fringe has been threaded.*

INSERTING EYELETS

Eyelets can be used to hold several layers of paper or card together; in addition they provide holes through which ribbon or string can be laced.

1 Glue the picture to the card, then place it on a block of wood. To make holes for the eyelets, place an eyelet punch in one corner of the picture and tap it sharply with a tack hammer. Repeat at each corner. Insert an eyelet into the first hole, through both picture and card.

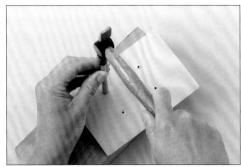

2 Turn the card over. Place the pointed end of the eyelet setter into the collar of the eyelet, and tap it sharply with a tack hammer. This will split and flatten the collar. Repeat for the remaining eyelets.

▶ *Outsize coloured metal eyelets threaded with string make an eye-catching trimming for a plain frame.*

Adding texture and ornament

Relief effects add subtle interest to a page. Embossed motifs can underline a theme and draw attention to the tactile quality of lovely paper, while glitter and sequins add a change of texture as well as sparkle. Use tiny beads or model your own motifs for three-dimensional embellishments.

BLIND (DRY) EMBOSSING

If you are using good paper with an interesting texture, embossed motifs make the most of its quality and lend an extra dimension to a layout.

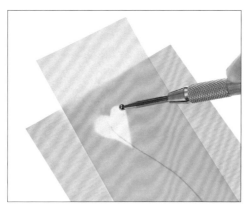

1 Draw your chosen motif on a piece of card (stock). Using a craft knife and working on a cutting mat, cut out the motif to make a stencil for embossing.

2 Place the stencil on a lightbox, if you have one, and lay a sheet of watercolour paper on top. Use an embossing tool to press into the paper, through the stencil. This is now the back of your paper. Reposition the paper to repeat the embossed motif as many times as required.

▲ *It's possible to use real objects as templates for embossed designs. On very smooth paper you could try a finely detailed object such as a coin, while on heavily textured paper greater relief is needed. Here, a flat scallop shell has been used to embossed rough handmade paper with a bold design.*

SHRINKING PLASTIC

1 Using felt-tipped pens, draw a design on the rough side of a piece of shrink plastic. If the plastic does not have a rough side, sand it lightly first with fine glass paper. The image should be no larger than 12.5 x 10cm/5 x 4in. Bear in mind that it will become seven times smaller and the colours will intensify.

2 Cut out the image, leaving a narrow border all round. Bake the plastic in an oven for a few minutes following the manufacturer's instructions. It will twist and turn then become flat. Remove the image, which will be pliable, and place a weight such as a book on top for a few moments to keep it flat while it cools and sets.

◀ *Embossed on thick, soft watercolour paper this simple heart motif gains complexity when repeated and overlapped in a soft curve, creating an engaging interplay of light and shade.*

GLITTER AND SEQUINS

If you want to add a little sparkle to a photograph, glitter paint is easy to control, allowing you to highlight fine details of the image. This product is particularly effective on black-and-white photographs.

1 Apply glitter paint to selected areas of a picture via the nozzle of the container or using a fine paintbrush.

2 Attach some small cabouchon jewellery stones to the glitter paint, using a pair of tweezers to position them accurately.

3 Gently drop sequins and sequin dust on the glitter paint. Shake off the excess.

RAISED (WET) EMBOSSING

In wet embossing, a design is stamped on the paper then coated with embossing powder, which is fused with the stamped design using heat to produce a raised motif. Embossing powders and inks are available in many colours as well as metallic and pearlized finishes.

1 Press the stamp into the ink pad and stamp an image on to the paper where required. While the ink is still wet, sprinkle embossing powder over the image. Make sure it is completely covered, then pour the excess powder back into the pot.

2 Use a dry paintbrush to gently brush away any excess embossing powder from the paper.

3 Switch on a heat gun. Holding it about 10cm/4in from the surface of the paper, gently blow heat over the embossing powder until it melts and flows together to make a raised image.

LOOSE GLITTER

Glitter needs to be attached to the paper using glue, usually painted on with a brush, so broad effects are easier to achieve than fine detail.

1 Using an old paintbrush, draw the design in PVA (white) glue. Sprinkle on the glitter.

2 Shake off the excess glitter on to a sheet of scrap paper then pour it back into the container.

BEADS

Small glass beads can be strung on thread using a beading needle or threaded on to fine wire: 0.4mm is a suitable thickness to use.

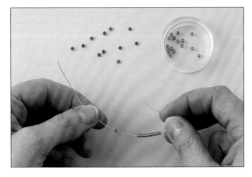

◀ Mount a photograph on card using spray adhesive. Resting on a cutting mat, use an awl to pierce holes at each end where you wish to add wires. Thread coloured wire up through one hole, bending back the end on the underside to keep the wire in place. Thread on a few beads. Insert the wire through the next hole. Bend back the wire to hold it in place on the underside, and snip off the excess with wirecutters. Repeat to attach wires between all the holes.

▲ *In this celebratory layout, coils of fine wire frame the pictures in the central panel.*

BEADED FLOWER

Glass rocaille beads are available in a range of exciting colours and add sparkle and colour to layouts. When threaded on wire they can be manipulated easily to make motifs.

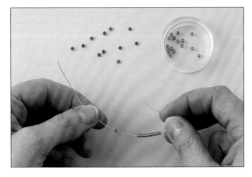

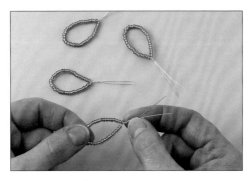

1 Bend back 3cm/1¼in of one end of a 12.5cm/5in length of fine wire to stop the beads slipping off. Thread on rocaille beads to a point 3cm/1¼in from the other end.

2 Twist the wire ends together under the beads to make a loop. Repeat to make four petals. Pierce the centre of a piece of card and poke the wire ends through the hole.

3 Stick the wire ends to the underside of the card with sticky tape. Splay the petals open on the front of the card and sew on a button to form the centre of the flower.

TASSELS

Little tassels made of silky thread are a charming trimming for elements such as small books containing journaling. They are quick and easy to make using embroidery thread (floss).

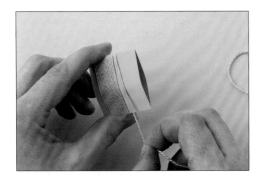

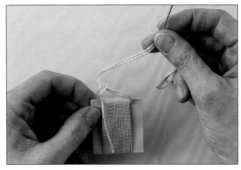

1 To make a tassel 4cm/1½in long, cut out a rectangle of card (card stock) measuring 8 x 4cm/3¼ x 1½in and fold it in half, parallel with the short edges. (Cut a larger rectangle of card to make a bigger tassel.) Bind thread around the card many times.

2 Fold a 40cm/16in length of thread in half and thread the ends through the eye of a large needle. Slip the needle behind the strands close to the fold then insert the needle through the loop of thread and pull tightly.

3 Slip the point of a scissor blade between the card layers and cut through the strands. Thread the needle with single thread and bind it tightly around the top of the tassel. Insert the needle into the tassel to lose the end of the thread. Trim the ends level.

Using modelling clay

Polymer and air-drying clays are ideal for moulding small three-dimensional motifs. Their fine texture enables you to create very detailed objects. Polymer clay needs to be baked in a domestic oven; air-drying clay hardens over about 24 hours. Glue motifs in place using strong epoxy glue.

CUTTING CLAY

For flat motifs, roll the clay out on a smooth cutting mat using a rolling pin. Rolling guides, such as two pieces of plywood placed on each side of the clay, guarantee an even thickness.

I Cut the clay with a craft knife. Cut straight edges against a metal ruler.

2 Use cookie cutters to stamp motifs then pull away the excess clay.

MAKING POLYMER CLAY MOTIFS

Complex motifs are easier to make if you first break the shapes down into a series of geometric forms, such as cylinders, cones, spheres and rectangles. These basic shapes can be pressed together and refined using modelling tools.

I To make a flower, roll a ball of polymer clay for the centre and six matching balls for the petals. Flatten all the balls and press the petals around the centre.

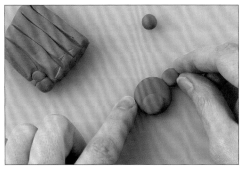

3 Roll a ball for a bear's head. and three smaller balls for the muzzle and ears. Flatten all the balls and press together. Impress the ears with the handle of an artist's brush.

2 Shape the petals by impressing them close to the flower centre using the pointed handle of an artist's brush.

4 Press on a tiny ball of black clay for the nose. Stamp the eyes with the glass head of a dressmaker's pin and use the point to indent a line down the muzzle.

STAMPING CLAY

For repeated motifs, flat shapes of polymer or air-drying clay can be stamped with any object with an interesting profile. Novelty buttons, for example, make good stamps. If the button has a shank, you can hold this to stamp the button into the clay. Bonsai wire (from specialist nurseries) is ideal for making wire stamping tools for curls and spirals as it is thick but very pliable.

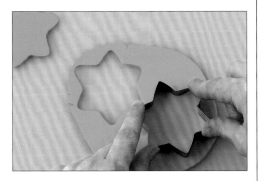

◀**I** To make a wire stamping tool, shape the wire using jewellery pliers. Bend the free end up at 90 degrees to form a handle.

▶ **2** Hold the handle and stamp the motif on to polymer or air-drying clay.

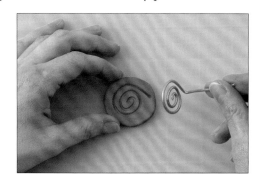

SEWING AND FABRICS

You can use fabrics and fibres of all kinds to add texture and variety to your album pages, and all can be enhanced with decorative stitching and embroidery, by hand or machine. Bold stitches also look good on paper and card (stock). If you are machine sewing on paper use a new needle.

STRAIGHT STITCH

Use plain machine stitching to join fabrics to paper or card (stock).

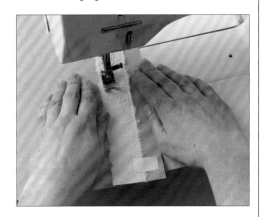

▲ For decorative effect or to apply a contrast coloured border, tear or cut a strip of paper or fabric. Tape it to the background with masking tape at the top and bottom. Stitch the strip with a straight stitch either in a straight line or meander in a wavy line. Remove the masking tape. Pull the thread ends to the wrong side and knot them. Cut off the excess thread.

ZIG-ZAG

In a contrasting colour, zig-zag stitch makes a decorative border.

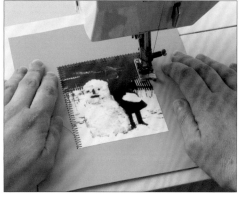

▲ Stick a photograph in place with paper glue. Stitch along the edges of the photo with a zig-zag stitch, pivoting the stitching at the corners. Pull the thread ends to the wrong side and knot them. Cut off the excess thread.

SATIN STITCH

Decorative lines of satin stitch can be worked on paper, card or fabric.

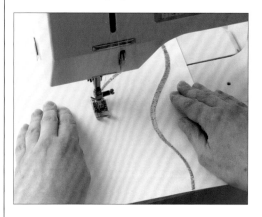

▲ To work a line of satin stitch on card (card stock) or fabric, gradually increase and decrease the width of the zig-zag stitch as you stitch. These lines are sewn with a shaded thread in random wavy lines. If you prefer, draw guidelines lightly with a pencil first. Pull the thread ends to the wrong side and knot them. Cut off the excess thread.

SATIN STITCH MOTIF

For a simple fabric motif, work the outline in satin stitch, using either matching or contrasting thread, then cut it out and attach with glue.

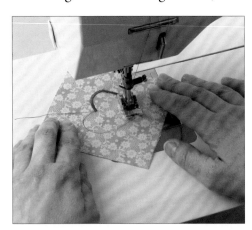

1 Draw the outline of the motif on fabric. Stitch along the line with a close zig-zag stitch, pivoting the stitching at any corners, until you return to the starting point. Pull the ends of the threads to the wrong side and knot them. Cut off the excess thread.

2 Use a pair of sharp embroidery scissors to cut away the fabric close to the stitching.

RUNNING STITCH

To keep your stitches perfectly even and avoid tearing paper or card (card stock), it's best to make the holes first using an awl.

1 Stick the photograph in place with paper glue. Resting on a cutting mat, pierce a row of holes along two opposite edges of the picture, using an awl or paper piercer.

2 Knot the end of a length of fine cord. Thread the cord in and out of the holes. Knot the cord on the last hole and cut off the excess. Repeat on the opposite edge.

GUIDE HOLES FOR HAND SEWING

Instead of piercing holes individually, try using your sewing machine, set to a long stitch length: the holes will be perfectly even and straight.

1 To create a frame or line of evenly spaced holes to sew through, first draw your design lightly with a pencil. Stitch with a straight stitch but no thread. Rub away the pencil marks with an eraser.

2 Sew in and out of the holes with thread. Knot the thread ends on the underside to start and finish. A photo or charm can be stuck within the frame.

CROSS STITCH

Use thick embroidery thread (floss) to make large-scale cross stitches.

1 Stick the photograph in position with spray adhesive and "sew" along the top and bottom edges with a row of large cross stitches using embroidery thread. To make it easier to sew, pierce a hole at each end of the cross with an awl, resting on a cutting mat. Knot the thread ends on the underside to start and finish.

▲ *A felt cover with a border of bold blanket stitching is a pretty treatment for a mini-album containing baby pictures.*

Working with fabric

A box of fabric scraps can be a real treasure trove when you are designing layouts. Materials such as net won't fray and looks lovely when gathered. Sheer organza is especially useful for subtle effects.

APPLIQUÉ

Bonding web is a fusible webbing used to apply fabric to fabric. It is simply ironed on, prevents fraying and is ideal for appliqué work.

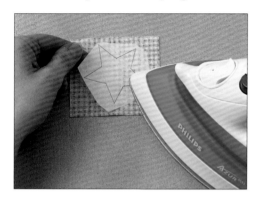

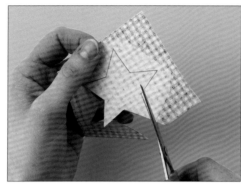

1 Draw your motif, in reverse if not symmetrical, on the paper backing of the bonding web. Roughly cut out the shape and iron it on to the wrong side of the fabric.

2 Cut out the design. Peel off the backing paper and position the motif right side up on the background. Press with a hot iron to fuse it in place. Oversew the edges by hand or with a machine satin stitch if you wish.

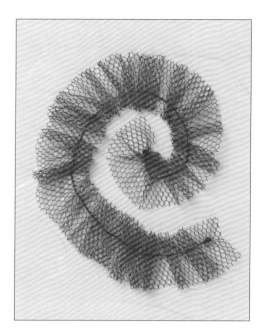

▲ *To make a pretty net spiral decoration, cut a 50 x 1.5cm/20 x ⅝in strip of net. Run a gathering thread along one long edge. Pull up the gathers until the strip is 15cm/6in long. Curl the strip and glue it in a spiral shape to your background using all-purpose household glue.*

ORGANZA LAYERS

This sheer fabric is available in many colours, some shot with silver or gold for exciting effects.

1 Cut a motif such as this tree from fabric or paper and stick it to the background card (card stock) with spray adhesive.

2 Tear strips of organza fabric. Use spray adhesive to stick the strips across the card overlapping or singly in bands. Trim the organza level with the edges of the card. Glue on sequins to complete the picture.

▶ *Sheer fabrics such as organza can be layered to create depth and interesting tonal effects. Here the raw edges also suggest grass.*

TIE-DYEING

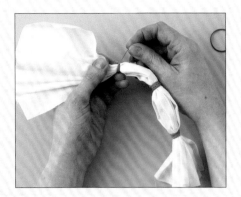

1 Wash and dry a piece of 100 per cent cotton fabric. Roughly gather the fabric in tight accordion folds and bind tightly with elastic bands where you want paler stripes in the design.

2 Dampen the fabric. Wearing protective gloves, plunge the fabric bundle into a bowl of cold water dye made up according to the manufacturer's instructions.

3 After the required soaking time, wash the fabric, rinse until the water runs clear, remove the bands and smooth it out to reveal the effect. Leave to dry then press with a hot iron.

NET SKIRT

A scrap of gathered net can be turned into a beautiful ballgown in no time.

▼ Cut a 14 × 6cm/5¹/₂ × 2¹/₂in rectangle of net. Gather one short edge tightly. Press a piece of iron-on interfacing to the wrong side of some matching fabric and cut out a bodice shape about 2.5cm/1in across. Glue the bodice and skirt to the background and attach a stick-on jewel at the waist.

RIBBON WEAVING

It's worth experimenting with ribbons of different widths to see what effects you can create. Once you're happy with the design, iron-on interfacing keeps it in place.

1 Cut a piece of iron-on interfacing to the finished size of your panel adding a 1cm/³/₈in margin at each edge. Matching the depth of the interfacing, cut enough lengths for the "warp" ribbons to fit along one edge. Lay them on the adhesive side of the interfacing and pin them in place along the top edge.

2 Cut enough lengths of contrasting "weft" ribbons to fit along one side edge. Weave the first ribbon in and out of the warp ribbons, passing it over one and under the next until you reach the opposite edge. Repeat to form a chequered pattern and pin all the ends in place.

▶ **3** Press the ribbons with a hot iron to fuse them to the interfacing, removing the pins as you work. Press the raw edges under.

◀ *A tiny evening dress, easily made from scraps of fabric, would make a romantic detail for a party or prom layout.*

LETTERING SKILLS

While pictures are the focal points of scrapbook layouts, titles, captions and written details are crucial to creating lasting souvenirs that keep your memories intact. Word-processing software and the thousands of available fonts enable you to establish a host of different moods and characters for your pages, but writing by hand stamps them with a unique personality – yours. Perfect calligraphy isn't essential, but practising a few of the techniques that go towards mastering this traditional skill can be helpful in improving the grace and legibility of your own handwriting.

BASIC PENMANSHIP

A broad nib, pen or brush is the essential tool for calligraphy. When you hold the pen in your hand the flat tip forms an angle to the horizontal writing line (called the pen angle). It takes some adjustment to use this sort of tool after using pointed pens and pencils, so practising basic strokes is helpful.

Writing position

To produce beautiful work you need a relaxed posture, so spend some time adjusting your position so that you are comfortable. You may like to work on a drawing board resting on a table top, or secured to the edge of a table so that the paper is on gentle slope. If you prefer, you can rest the board on your lap, or flat on a table, resting your weight on your non-writing arm so that you have free movement with your pen.

Remember to place some extra sheets beneath the paper you are working on to act as padding: this will help the flexibility of the nib and stop it scratching the paper and spattering ink. Attach the writing sheets securely to the board with masking tape.

Light should fall evenly on your working area; although good daylight is best, you can also use an adjustable lamp to light the page.

Terminology

Calligraphy uses special terms to describe the consituent parts of letters and words and the way they are written. The style or "hand" in which the writing is created is composed of "letterforms". These are divided into capital, or "upper-case" letters and smaller "lower-case" letters. Most text is written in the latter because they are easier to read than solid blocks of capitals.

The "x-height" is the height of the full letter in capitals or the main body of

◄ *Calligraphy pens are available with different size nibs. This type of pen can be used with different colours and consistencies of ink.*

small letters, excluding "ascenders" and "descenders", which extend above or below the line of the text.

Calligraphers use pencil guidelines to ensure that their strokes are correctly placed on the page, and the two most important are those drawn to mark the top and bottom of the x-height.

Forming strokes

When you write with a normal pen, it can easily be moved round the page. When you are using a calligraphy pen this is not possible because the nib resists against the paper and may cause an ink blot or mark. For this reason, letters are made from several separate strokes, lifting the pen between them. For example, the letter "o" is made using two strokes, with one pen lift, while a small "d" is made in three strokes and other letters may require four. Practise slowly to start with.

WRITING WITH THE LEFT HAND

If you are left-handed you should sit to the right of the paper and tuck the left elbow into the waist, twisting the wrist so as to hold the pen at the required angle. Special left-oblique nibs are available to minimize the amount that the wrist needs to be bent, but if you can manage with straight-edged nibs the left-hander will have a greater choice of nibs available to them.

Three strokes   Four strokes

PRACTICE STROKES

To begin with it is helpful to practise just keeping the whole nib edge against the paper.

Practise simple curves and angles before you form any letters. Zig-zag patterns will show you the thinnest and thickest marks the nib is capable of.

PEN ANGLES

Holding the pen at the same angle to the writing line for every letter is an essential discipline to create letters that work well together. Practise first on spare paper. A line of differently angled letters will look odd.

Resist the temptation to move the wrist as you would in standard writing. As you complete each letter, check that you are keeping the same pen angle: it is easy to

change without noticing. Zig-zag patterns, made at the correct angle for the alphabet you are using, can be a useful warming up exercise before writing.

LAYING OUT TEXT

Having decided what you are going to write, you need to plan where each word will fall and work out how much space it will take up, so that the page looks balanced and harmonious. Think about the relative importance of titles – and hence which will be larger or smaller.

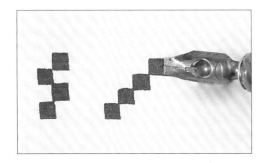

1 Determine the x-height of an alphabet using a "ladder" of nib widths. Holding the nib at 90 degrees to the baseline, make a clear mark, then move the pen up and repeat for the required number of widths.

2 Measure the height of the ladder and use this measurement to mark the x-height down both sides of the paper, then join the marks up with a ruler and pencil. If you have a T-square you can mark one side only.

3 When ruling guidelines for lower-case letters, leave the equivalent of two x-heights between each line of text to allow for ascenders and descenders. For capitals, you can leave one x-height or even less.

4 When you are going to write mostly in lower case with the occasional capital, rule as for lower case and gauge the height of the capital letters by eye.

Unspaced ▼
Spaced ▼

5 Once you start writing, it is important to be aware of letter spacing and awkward combinations, such as the "r" and "a" above: move them closer to create a natural space.

6 Adjusting letter spacing helps to make the text more legible by evening out the frequency of downstrokes: leave more space between adjacent uprights, as above.

Foundational hand

To grasp the principles of calligraphy it is best to start by learning an alphabet. The Foundational, or Round, hand was devised by the British calligrapher Edward Johnston (1872–1944), who is credited with reviving the art of penmanship and lettering in the modern age.

▶ *The numerals and letters of the alphabet are written in a specific order. Follow the numbers on the digits and letters opposite to achieve the best effect.*

The Foundational hand is simply crafted, based on the circle made by two overlapping strokes of the pen, and is written with a constant pen angle of 30 degrees and few pen lifts. It is the constant angle that produces the characteristic thick and thin strokes of the letterforms. Johnston based his design for the lower-case letters on the Ramsey Psalter, a late tenth-century English manuscript now in the British Library. The capitals, however, are based on carved letterforms used in ancient Rome, and their elegant proportions relate to the geometry of a circle within a square.

The basic rules

Foundational hand is a formal, upright script, in which each letter is made up of two or more strokes. The letters should be evenly spaced for easy reading. An important characteristic of this hand is that the top curves of "c" and "r" are slightly flattened to help the eye travel along the line of writing.

The x-height is four nib-widths. Turn the pen sideways to make four adjacent squares with the nib, then rule your guidelines that distance apart. The ascenders and descenders should be less than three-quarters of the x-height (two or three nib-widths). The capital letters should be just two nib-widths above the x-height and do not look right if they are any higher. Hold the nib at a constant angle of 30 degrees for all letters except for diagonals, where the first stroke is made with a pen angle of 45 degrees.

Practice exercises

Almost all the letterforms of this hand relate to the circle and arches, so practise by drawing controlled crescent moon shapes, beginning and ending on a thin point. These semicircles can then be attached to upright stems to create rounded letterforms, or they can be extended into a downstroke to form arches. Begin high up and inside the stem to create a strong, rounded arch. Rounded serifs are used on entry and exit strokes to embellish the letters.

GROUPS

Round or circular

Note where the thin parts of the letters are. The first stroke of these letters should be a clean semicircular sweep, producing a shape like a crescent moon. Start at the top and move the pen downwards. The left and right edges of the pen form the circles.

Arched

The arch joins the stem high up. Beginning with the pen in the stem, draw outwards in a wide curve, following the "o" form. Start the letters with a strong, curved serif and end with a smaller curved serif. Keep the pen angle at 30 degrees throughout.

Diagonal

For the first stroke, hold the pen at the steeper angle of 45 degrees. This will prevent the stroke from being too thick. Take care not to make any curve on this stroke. Revert to a pen angle of 30 degrees for the second stroke.

Ungrouped

Keep the pen angle at 30 degrees for these letters. Follow the smooth shape of the "o" when drawing curves. Crossbars should sit just below the top line, and should protrude to nearly the width of the curve.

STROKES
(1st = red, 2nd= blue, 3rd = green)

The letter "o" is made by two overlapping semicircular strokes, which produce the characteristic oval shape inside the letter. The back of the "e" does not quite follow the "o", but is flattened so it appears balanced. The top joins just above halfway.

For "a" draw an arch continuing into a straight stroke. The bowl begins halfway down the stem. The "u" follows the same line as an "n" but upside down, producing a strong arch with no thin hairlines. Add the stem last.

Start the ascender for "k" three nib-widths above the x-height. The second stroke is a continuous movement forming a right-angle. The pen angle is steepened for the first stroke of "v" and the second begins with a small serif. The two should sit upright.

The base of the first stroke of the "j" curves inwards to cup the preceeding letter "i". The second begins with a small serif and joins the base. The dot above the j is formed last. Start the "t" above the top line. The crossbar forms the second stroke, just below the top line.

1 2 3 4 5 6 7 8 9 0

A B C D E F G
H I J K L M N
O P Q R S T U
V W X Y Z & Æ

a b c d e f g
h i j k l m n
o p q r s t u
v w x y z &

? æ ě ŭ é ß .,;:

DIGITAL SCRAPBOOKING

There is a whole range of software available for digital scrapping. Some of the programs that came free with your computer, printer or digital camera, such as simple layout software, or image-viewing and editing programs, are essential scrapbooking tools. Specific digital scrapbooking software is also available and is easy to use to import photographs and design elements to your pages. For those wishing to work at an advanced level, professional image-editing software enables you to create a vast range of effects on photographs and layouts.

SCRAPBOOKING SOFTWARE

If you enjoy scrapbooking and also like working on a computer, you will enjoy all the possibilities of creativity offered by designing your scrapbook pages on screen. Being able to undo, redo, or make several different versions of your ideas and see them side by side without wasting any paper, is a joy. Your computer and printer, with various software packages, give you all the basics you need to design and print great pages. If you also have a scanner, digital camera and access to the internet you will have even more creative options. There are many scrapbooking websites, which offer a variety of e-papers, borders and embellishments at high resolution, allowing you to make good-quality prints. They sell templates and even ready-made pages – so all you need to do is position your photos.

Each site has its own style: some elements look very high-tech and computer generated, whereas others have a more traditional feel. If you need inspiration you can browse through the galleries on the sites, which are full of exciting ideas. There are many software tutorials to help you out, too.

▼ *Scrapbooking websites such as scrapgirls.com offer themed collections of background designs, overlays, embellishments, and everything you need to compile your digital pages.*

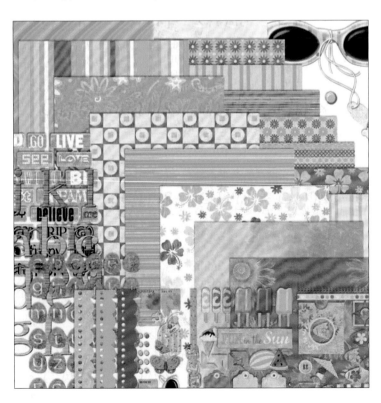

CREATING DIGITAL PAGES

Even the most basic software can be used to create backgrounds and make different shapes and frames to contain photographs and journaling. You can either use these in traditional scrapbook layouts by printing all the elements individually to arrange together on paper, or print the finished page. You can buy a whole range of papers to print on, and experiment with coloured and textured papers, and even fabric.

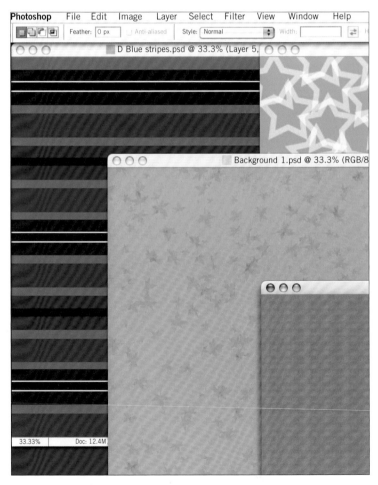

I To begin your page using image-editing software such as Photoshop, set the design area to 30 × 30cm/12 × 12in (it can later be reduced to 20 × 20cm/8 × 8in if you want to print on to A4 paper). For good printing quality use 300dpi (dots per inch) when creating and importing images, and experiment with different filters and effects. The stripes on the left were achieved by colouring rectangles then repeating down the page.

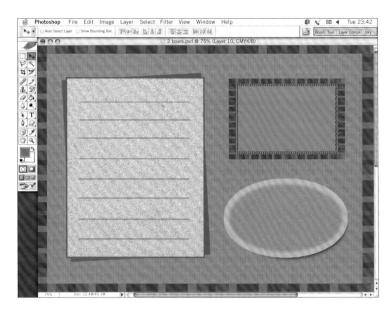

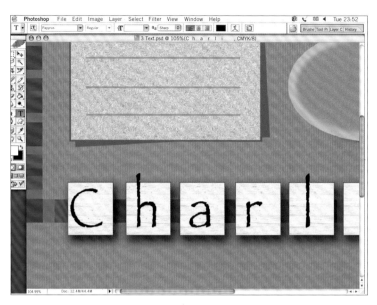

2 Squares, circles, stars and more can be created to make boxes, borders and embellishments, then coloured and treated with different filters and effects. Here the striped background has been used to create a stripy border. In the journaling panel on the left, a textured surface and rules imitate notepaper. The shape was duplicated then twisted a little and re-coloured to give a shadow effect. Another shadow under the oval shape gives it a three-dimensional feel. You can resize and reshape the elements as much as you like, until you are happy with the basic layout.

3 The beauty of creating journal boxes on screen is that you can type your story straight into the box, and then edit it and resize the type or the box until everything fits beautifully and you have exactly the look you want to achieve. Your computer will come with a basic range of fonts installed, and many more are available if you want to create a particular look. They can be enlarged, emboldened, italicized and capitalized and all will look different. Special effects for titles and other text include drop shadows, 3-D effects and outline lettering, and you can of course type in any colour to fit the mood of the layout. Alternatively, you can print the empty boxes and write the text by hand for a traditional look, or print your text on clear film and superimpose it on a printed background.

DRAWING A SOLID OBJECT

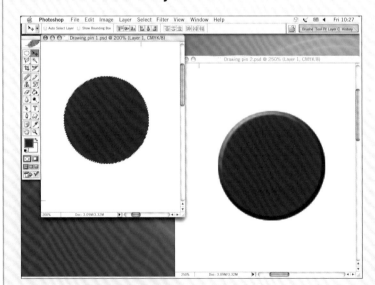

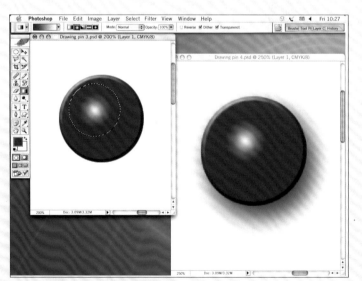

1 Try using imaging software to create the illusion of solid objects such as this drawing pin (thumb tack). Create a circle and colour it, using the eyedropper tool to pick a colour from one of your photos. Create a bevel edge using the Bevel and Emboss layer style. Here a smooth inner bevel has been added with a shading angle of 120 degrees. Play with the settings until you are happy with the effect.

2 To add a little shine to the surface of the pin, create a smaller circle on the surface. Choose Radial Gradient in the gradient tool menu and scale to make the area of shine as big or small as you want it. Here it has been set at 56 degrees. Finally add a shadow to relate the pin to the background, at the same angles of 120 degrees. You can now scale the image down to a realistic size and use it to "pin" your photograph to the page.

Scanning and using digital images

A scanner is definitely useful if you have an archive of traditional photographs you want to scrapbook digitally. All your old family photos can be scanned too, so all your relatives can have their own copies. As well as photographic prints, both colour and black and white, most scanners can also be used to copy transparencies and negatives. And of course your traditional paper scrapbook pages can be scanned, to be stored or refined digitally, or emailed to your friends.

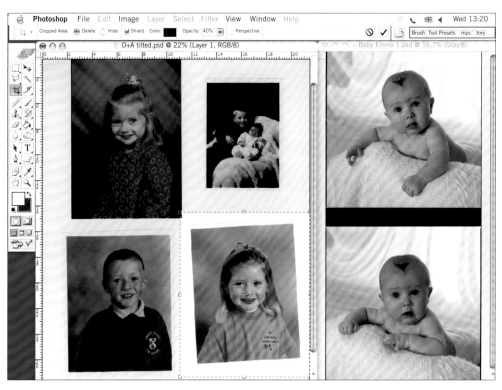

Making a scan

1 Fit as many photos on to the scanner bed as possible, as they can be cropped individually once they are scanned. Work at 300dpi or, for small photos that you may want to use at, say, three times the original size, at 900dpi. Save and name the scan.

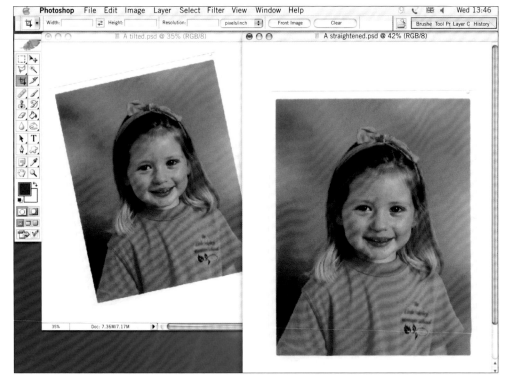

2 Crop out the picture you want to use, and save and rename it as a separate file. If the picture is a bit wonky, which often happens when scanning prints, or even upside down, it can be turned around easily in increments of 90 degrees or less, until it is straight. Check the alignments using the guides on the screen.

DIGITAL PHOTO FILES

If you have a digital camera, all your photographs can be downloaded straight to your computer using the software supplied with the camera. The pictures are then ready to use on digital scrapbook pages, or can be printed to use traditionally. Store each set of digital photos in a folder and label as you would ordinary prints.

You can store your photographs, and other scrapbooking material, on your computer, but they will take up a lot of memory. You should certainly delete any bad pictures so they do not take up valuable space, and it is best to copy all your pictures on to CDs or DVDs, so that you have back-up copies.

Use your camera for backgrounds such as beach, grass and sky, as well as other elements such as signs, tickets, labels and buttons. With these and elements from other sources you can build up a library of digital papers, embellishments and typography to use whenever you want.

NOW TRY THIS

1 Scan your photograph. Add a white border to imitate a print, by increasing the canvas size, before you bring it on to the album page. Duplicate the image box, twist by a few degrees, re-colour and put behind the photograph to give the semi-shadow effect.

2 Create stripes for the background, matching colours from the photo using the eyedropper tool.

3 Take a patch of colour from the photo background to use for the decorative boxes to the right of the photograph. Reshape one of these boxes to add the cross bands at the bottom and right of the page.

4 Create individual text boxes with shadows and add type to create the title.

5 You can make the drawing pins (thumb tacks) digitally as here, or print the page and then add buttons and other three-dimensional embellishments to the printed version. For best results use a good quality printing paper, and allow plenty of time for the inks to dry.

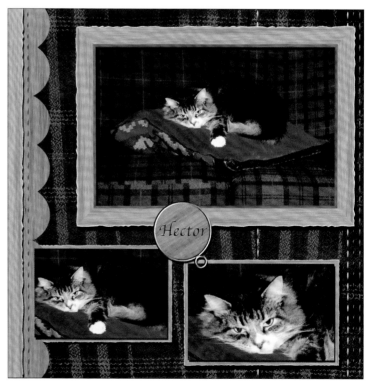

▲ The denim dungarees Jack is wearing in the colour photograph provided the inspiration for this layout. The background is a picture of the garment itself, digitally augmented with stripes and lettering, and the photograph has been vignetted in a shape that fits neatly on to the pocket.

▲ A single scanned photograph of this pampered pet on his favourite cushion has been used three times at different scales, and the tartan rug in the picture also forms the background design. Don't forget that you can use a scanner to create digital images of fabrics and printed papers as well as photographs. The frames, name tag and stitching are all digital embellishments.

USING A SCANNER FOR SPECIAL EFFECTS

As well as creating digital images from your photographic prints and negatives, you can use a scanner like a camera to create pictures of a whole host of other items that you might want to use on your scrapbook page. Different patterns and textures for backgrounds, traditional embellishments such as buttons, bows, lace, ribbon or photo corners can all be scanned to be used on your pages. All those tickets and other ephemera from your travels can be scanned in to go with the photos. In fact, if you can pick it up, then you can usually scan it! The flatter the item, the better the scan.

▲ *Woven fabric, denim from a pair of jeans, a piece of knitwear, flower petals and a child's painting have been scanned here. Fabric needs to be pulled taut across the scanner bed to avoid creases, unless of course you are after a creased effect. As with photographs, you can crop around the area that you want to use after making the scan. The scans can be used as they are, or layers, colours and other effects can be added to tone them down, creating more abstract patterns.*

1 Create a border around the knitwear background by duplicating the background, cutting out a row of stitching, copying this to the other side, then copying and rotating to make the other two sides of the square. Use the same method to make the edging around the photograph.

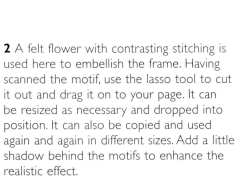

2 A felt flower with contrasting stitching is used here to embellish the frame. Having scanned the motif, use the lasso tool to cut it out and drag it on to your page. It can be resized as necessary and dropped into position. It can also be copied and used again and again in different sizes. Add a little shadow behind the motifs to enhance the realistic effect.

▲ *The final touch to this pretty layout is a row of simple felt shapes embroidered with the letters of the child's name. The pink knitted frame is a good match for this photograph, but you could of course change the colour if you wanted to use this texture in a different context.*

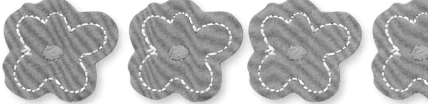

IMPROVING YOUR PHOTOS

Once you have your photos in digital format, there are a number of easy ways to enhance the quality of both black and white and colour photographs. Even the most basic picture-editing software packages will allow you to improve the colour or composition, or restore damaged prints. Always make a copy of the original scan to work on, so that you can refer back to it or start again if you don't like the new effect.

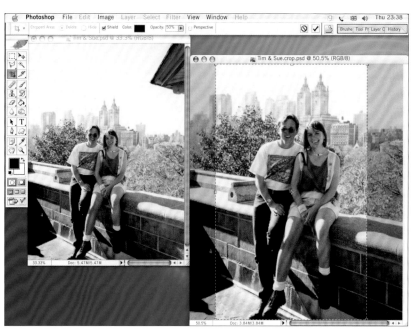

Cropping out distracting objects

If you find you have an awkward or distracting object in the background, or foreground, like this overhanging roof, it can often easily be cropped out using the crop or selection tool. Experiment with cropping even further to focus more on the subjects.

Improving colour

Here the picture on the left is too light and the contrast and colour have been improved using the automatic settings. To refine the result further you could alter the contrast and brightness controls manually, and add the colours individually in the colour balance panel.

Improving the sky

A featureless or dull sky is easily improved. First select the sky area using the wand or lasso tool. Select a suitable sky colour to go with the foreground, then select linear gradient in the gradient tool. Draw a vertical line with the mouse to add the gradient colour – the longer the line the more colour there will be in the background. Experiment with the gradient until you are happy with it.

Retouching

If you don't want to crop into the background of a picture, you may be able to remove a distracting object by retouching. Use the clone tool initially, to delete the object and match the area with the rest of the background. Then use the healing brush to soften any harsh edges. This method can be used to eliminate red eye, too.

Making a focal point

You can blur the background if it is too distracting and you want to focus attention on the subject. Use the lasso tool to draw around the subject and make a clipping path. Invert the path to make the background the working area. Now choose Radial Blur in the filter menu. Decide how much blur to apply and position the blur centre: in this case it has been moved down below the centre of the image so that the effect circulates around the subjects.

CHOOSING AND VIEWING PHOTOGRAPHS

Photo-viewing software is often supplied with your camera, printer or computer. It allows photographs to be imported from a digital camera and then viewed as large or small as needed. Viewing a group of photographs together as thumbnails makes it easier to make the best selection for a scrapbook page. You can arrange your picture library in folders or albums and add titles. Some software allows you to do a little picture editing too. You can rotate photos to view them the right way round, crop to improve framing and even create a slideshow. You can also import your finished digital pages to be viewed as a slideshow.

IMPROVING BLACK-AND-WHITE PHOTOGRAPHS

As with colour photographs, black-and-white pictures can easily be improved with the addition of special effects.

Brightening dark pictures

If a photograph is too dark, as on the left, make it brighter using the brightness control and lessen the contrast to lighten it. Use the curves and levels controls to refine the image. The sharpness can be improved too, which can be helpful with some older photos.

Repairing creases and tears

When old photos have been stored for a long time, they may be creased or damaged. They may also be stained and spotted with damp or mould. The clone tool and the healing brush are both easy to use to retouch any damaged areas, and tears, spots and even small holes can be repaired very effectively.

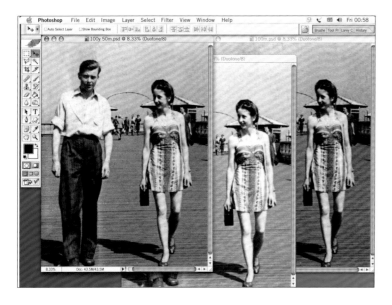

Creating tints and duotones

Copy the image (converting to greyscale if it is colour) then choose Duotone from the image menu. This allows you to create the photo in two, three or even four colours of your choice. Be careful – some colours, such as green, can make a photo look strange. Warm sepia works well with old photos. The duotones above show the effects created using orange (100y, 100m), yellow (100y) and finally magenta (100m).

Eliminating creased corners

Old photos often have creased or bent corners. If the damage is too bad to retouch in the digital version, you could try this effect. Draw an oval shape around the subject, then invert the selection so the background is selected and delete it. The edge of the photo is softened, or vignetted, by feathering, in this case by 30 pixels, before hitting delete. This gives a soft, period feel to the picture.

NOW TRY THIS

1 Scan a sheet of brown paper for the background. Add brush marks around the edges to create the effect of antique paper.

2 Add a white border to the photo, by increasing the canvas size before you bring it on to the page. Position it on the page, resizing to fit. Add a rectangular text box below and add the title.

3 Make a tag, or download a tag from a scrapbooking website. Position it at an angle in the corner of the page. Select a rectangular section of the tag. Copy this and enlarge it down the left side of the page. Tone down the colour by adding a semi-opaque layer over it.

4 Scan in photo corners, paper reinforcements and ribbon. Position the paper reinforcements, then add the ribbon as if threaded through them. Resize and crop to fit. Duplicate the ribbon and position it over the tag. Twist it around until it looks right and crop the length a bit. Add the photo corners. Finally, add a little shadow to all the elements to give a three-dimensional effect.

Dan & Joan

▲ *The photograph of New York used as the background was given a painted effect using Fresco in the filter menu. In the main photo, Ink Outlines was used for the distant view, and Glass Distort noise effect has been added around the edge to soften it. A variety of city scenes have been added around the edges of the page to enhance the mood.*

CREATING A PHOTOGRAPHIC BACKGROUND

Photographic backgrounds can be very effective provided they don't distract too much attention from the main subject. There are many ways to avoid this, such as keeping the background to a solid colour, reducing the opacity of the background image, throwing it out of focus or applying a filter.

I Duplicate the background layer twice. On the top layer create a box around the area to be full strength, invert and crop out the background. You can check the crop by just viewing that layer. If you want to soften the edges, feather the crop.

2 Click on the layer below. Reduce the opacity, or strength, of the background in the layers menu until you get the effect you want: in this case the background has an opacity of 60 per cent.

3 To enhance the subject further, enlarge the full-strength area. Here this was subtly done by keeping the edge of the grass in line with the background. A soft shadow was added to lift it off the page.

CREATING A PANORAMA AND MONTAGE

Various programs are available to stitch panoramas together, but you can do this yourself. It works best if the pictures are taken from the same standpoint.

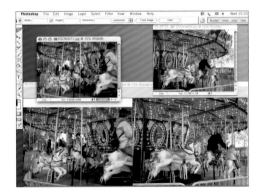

I If you have an assortment of photos, choose the ones that match up best. Bring them on to the same page, resize as necessary and nudge along to find the best match. Enlarge the canvas to accommodate the photos.

2 To add people to the scene, cut them out using the lasso tool, and move across to the panorama. They can be flipped, rotated and resized to fit. Use this method to add as many images as you need.

3 After adding all the images and adjusting them to fit into the scene, look at the edge of the final photo. If it is uneven it can be cropped, and the page area altered so that it fits a page or across a spread.

CREATING A TORN PAPER EFFECT

Torn paper is a good effect to master for use in your digital scrapbook pages. A real piece of paper can be torn and scanned, but it may not be quite the right shape. You can learn to alter the shape and size of a real paper scan or you can create a mock effect. Once you know how to create the effect with your software, this method can be used on any shape you need.

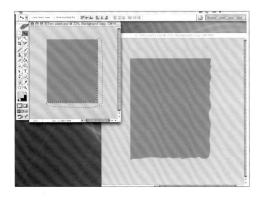

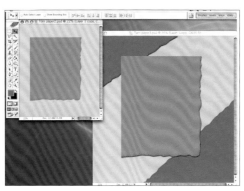

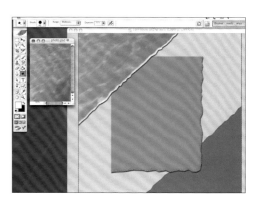

1 Create and colour a rectangle. Make a jagged line around two sides with the lasso tool. Join up the shape and hit delete.

2 Add noise in the filters menu and adjust the levels, making the torn area lighter or darker to suit your needs. This gives a jagged torn edge effect on two sides of the rectangular sheet.

3 This effect can be added to the edge of a photograph. Apply the torn paper method as described in steps 1 and 2, then use the dodge tool along the jagged edge so that it appears white like a tear in a real print.

CREATING A CALENDAR

Once you are into digital scrapbooking it is very easy to create your own calendar, adding seasonal effects. Scrapbooking websites offer many different calendar templates. Some can be created on the website and then downloaded to print (you will need broadband for this). Others are just like digital scrapbook templates and can be downloaded and designed as usual.

1 For this October page, create an autumn background from leaf-patterned paper with an opaque layer over it to soften the colour. Add numbered boxes, duplicating the required amount. Add the days of the week above each column.

2 Import the photos, resizing and moving them around until you are happy with the composition. Using the eyedropper to pick out a dark colour from one of the photos, add a border and shadows to both pictures.

3 Add a contrasting band at the top by creating a rectangular box and using the eyedropper to colour it. Add noise to create texture and place it behind the top of the upper photo. Duplicate the band and position one at the bottom of the page. Duplicate again and position the middle band across the foot of the lower photo.

4 Position the word "October" along the middle band, and add a shadow so that it stands out. Finally, using the leafy brush, spatter a few leaves in the bottom corner.

UPLOADING PAGES

Having made your digital page, you can save it to disc for posterity, and print as many copies as you like. The brilliant thing about digital pages is that you can also email them to friends, and even upload them on to one of the many websites that allow you to show them. If your pages are saved at 300dpi you should first reduce the resolution to 72dpi. This generally makes your page small enough to be emailed and uploaded on to the web. Follow the instructions given on the website for uploading your material for display.

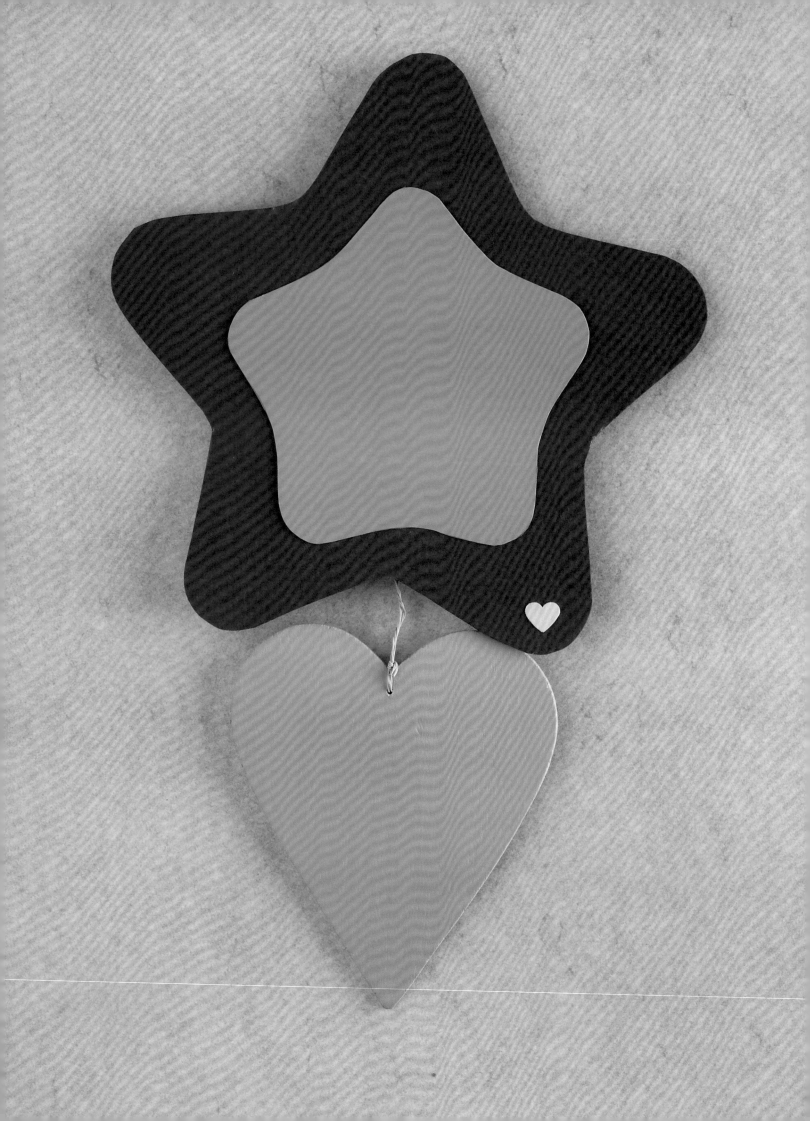

Styles to suit

For inspiration for the style of your scrapbook pages you need generally look no further than the photographs you want to display and your knowledge of their subjects. So while a collection of old family photographs, for instance, might seem to warrant a "traditional" treatment, your partying forebears enjoying their cocktails might look happier in chic Art Deco black and silver frames to echo their sharp suits and stylish dresses.

The fun is in relating your backgrounds and decorations to the contents of the pictures, and it's important that the photographs always have a starring role: the thousands of patterns and ornaments available from scrapbooking stores should never be allowed to overwhelm the personal elements of your displays.

Keeping it traditional

The photograph albums and scrapbooks of earlier generations have a wonderfully evocative look. It can be fun to adopt their look, either with squared up presentations of photographs, or with a twist, by adding in memorabilia that has been digitally scanned or enhanced. Keep the presentation quite formal, with the pictures squarely mounted in narrow borders or in old-fashioned photo corners, and add handwritten captions.

▼ *This page crowded with lots of tickets and other bits and pieces evokes the eventful days of a memorable trip to San Francisco. It has been digitally created, and makes use of the standard elements of a traditional scrapbook.*

▶ *Although created digitally, this layout looks back to an earlier era with its metal corners and hand-tinted black and white pictures.*

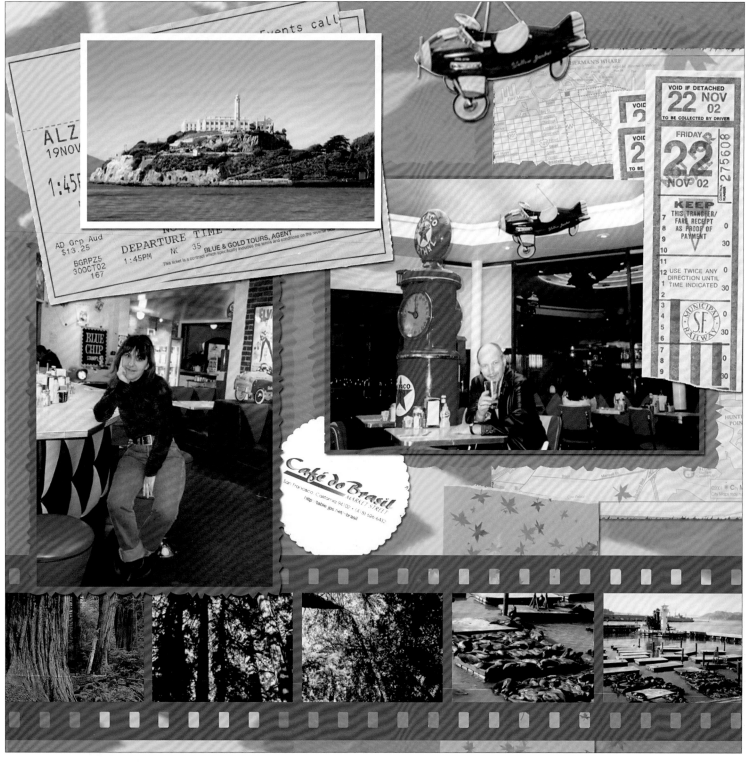

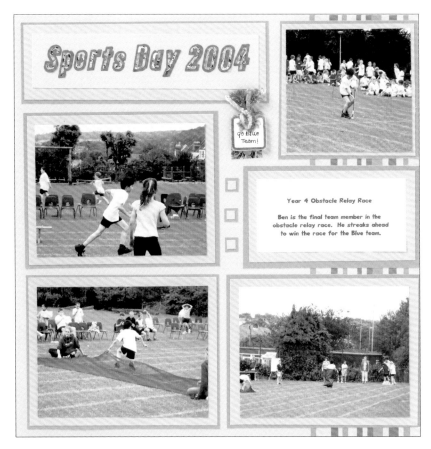

▲ *The camouflage theme is taken from the uniforms in the picture and the titling and black border give a period feel.*

▲ *Here the pictures telling the story of the children's race almost fill the page, apart from a small panel describing what happened, and are squarely arranged with little embellishment.*

▶ *The dog's formal pose in this photograph has inspired an equally formal presentation in a double frame with bound corners.*

▼ *This record of a day at the zoo uses matching frames for all the pictures. The string detail is based on old album bindings.*

▲ *An old map has been used as the background to this Caribbean beach scene and neatly imitates the look of the sand where the boat sits in readiness to head out to sea.*

Bold graphics

Crisp geometric shapes and repeating patterns can make really effective settings for strong images, or if you are using digital images, you could make a feature of the graphics within the photograph by repeating and blurring edges.

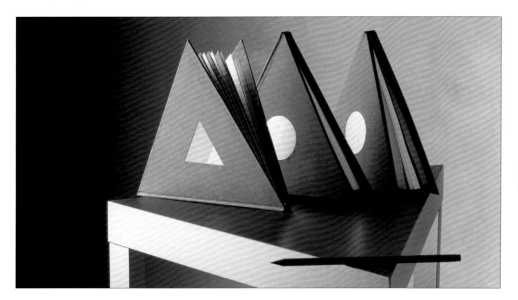

▲ *To create a smart, unified look for a multivolume set of family albums, go for matching or co-ordinated bindings in formal designs. Choose colours that suit your home décor so you'll want to have them on show.*

▲ *Albums need not be square: these striking triangular volumes have an Oriental feel and demand a modern, minimalist treatment on the pages inside.*

▶ *Papers printed in strong graphic designs like these make wonderful album covers. If you want to mix them up, look for designs of equal strength and scale, or use the same motifs in different sizes or colours.*

▼ *Die-cut patterns create a strong graphic effect when they are set against a background in a contrasting colour, as in this pretty ribbon-tied folder.*

▲ Although the carousel is a very traditional subject, the modern technique of digital splicing has resulted in an image that forces you to take a second look.

◄ Image-editing software has been used to add some eye-catching stripes to this digitally created scrapbook page.

▼ Royalty-free images from old black and white engravings can be photocopied and added to paper collages to make lovely album covers, cards and gift tags.

Fabric and stitch

If you are skilled with a needle, there are lots of creative ways to introduce textiles and stitching into your scrapbooking, from embroidered album covers to painted or printed silk panels or braided embellishments.

▼ *A small embroidery can become a front cover feature of a special album cover. This motif would be appropriate for a gardener.*

▶ *This small-scale book cover has been made by appliquéing small squares to a background fabric and satin stitching the raw edges.*

▲ Thick woven cotton or linen makes a
lovely album cover, trimmed with
embroidered titling and decorative blanket
stitch and closed with two buttoned bands.

◄ For a contemporary decoration for the
front of an album cover stitch small strips of
evenly-spaced brightly coloured silk fabrics in
a column to one side.

► Use transfer paper to copy a favourite
photo on to fine fabric such as silk to form
the centrepiece of an appliquéd panel.

Heritage

Most families have collections of photographs and ephemera handed down from previous generations, and it can be very rewarding to identify and mount them in albums to preserve them for the future. Good heritage layouts can be powerful evocations of the period when the pictures were taken.

▼ *Copies of letters to home and other contemporary memorabilia make moving additions to wartime pages.*

▲ *Try to get older relatives to help you identify the subjects of photographs in your old family albums.*

◀ *Treasured souvenirs of long-ago trips deserve to be properly displayed and preserved for the future.*

▼ *A decorative collage in period style can make the most of simple but precious family snaps.*

▲ When you're assembling a family group like this, the photographs themselves may all be simple portraits, but with personal knowledge of the subjects of the pictures you can choose appropriate backgrounds that help to show what the people were really like.

▼ For old photographs that are to be out on display, use old materials in muted colours to frame them. Here an antique cream piece of card (stock) immediately frames the photograph, and the outer frame is made from coloured corrugated cardboard, which picks up the darkest tones in the photograph.

▲ If you've inherited old family albums they're likely to be crammed with small black and white or sepia prints. It can be effective to reflect some of that style in your new album, but it's often possible to improve the images greatly by scanning and enhancing faded prints and reprinting them on a larger scale.

Natural inspiration

Don't forget your scrapbook when you're out and about: as well as bringing home photographs, gather natural objects such as shells, leaves and flowers that will help you build up a complete picture of the places you visited.

▲ *This display box is a lovely way to bring together a photograph of a happy day on the beach with the collection of seashells you made while you were there.*

◄ *Instead of portraying a particular place, water has been chosen as the theme for this layout, bringing together diverse natural scenes. However, all the photographs used were taken in similar weather conditions, so the colours give the page a very unified feel.*

▼ *Handmade paper makes the perfect cover for an album on a natural theme. This sheet incorporates delicate scattered flower petals, and pressed flowers have been used to decorate the title panel. A simple undyed raffia tie holds it all together.*

▲ *This cover, decorated with a collage of leaves and flowers and bound with string, would be perfect for an album recording a garden tour.*

Cardigan Castle 2004

▲ The complex frame-within-a-frame used in this layout, combined with the unusual view in the photograph, creates the effect of a window opening in the page, through which you can see the view of the tree beyond. The embellishment of leafy twigs is clearly related to the picture.

St Agnes

▲ As well as taking photographs of views and landscapes when you're on holiday, you can use your camera to record interesting abstract images and close-ups for fantastic borders and backgrounds in future scrapbooks.

◀ Pretty pressed flowers form the focal point on this handmade album cover. The cover is made from textured paper, which has a handmade quality to it. The flowers can be collected fresh in spring and summer and pressed at home.

▼ Trinket boxes are a delightful way to store small treasures that are unsuitable for your album pages because of their shape. Beautify plain boxes with patterned papers and embellishments such as pressed flowers and leaves.

Simple colour schemes

A monochrome treatment is an obvious choice for a collection of black-and-white photographs, but it can also be extremely effective with pictures in which the colour range is fairly limited. Don't limit your ideas to black and white but explore other single colours that match or contrast well with your images.

▼ *A delicately decorated photograph box makes an elegant minimal presentation for a silver wedding souvenir.*

◄ *Although these striking seascapes are in colour the effect is almost monochromatic, and the simple black and white layout suits them perfectly.*

▼ *A crowded layout including photographs of all the members of a family is full of interest, and keeping it all in black and white gives a simple, graphic look.*

▲ *This all-white frame is intricately designed and texturally interesting, but doesn't distract attention from the photograph inside.*

▼ *Paper printed with a toile de Jouy design goes well with a strong collection of black-and-white photographs, though the plain black background is needed to keep all the images clear and well defined. The effect is softened with a purple border and ribbons.*

◄ *A fragile collection of old sepia prints can be overpowered by stark black-and-white or any strong colours, and looks best with gentle, faded tones.*

▲ *A photographic background, such as this drift of rose petals created for a wedding album, can have its opacity level reduced and be printed in just one or two colours, so that it does not compete visually with the photographs on the pages.*

◄ *In many older photograph albums the pages are of matt black paper, and this can still make a very effective and dramatic setting for both black and white and colour prints.*

▲ *A white wedding album luxuriously bound in white leather or vellum demands perfectly matted prints and a restrained approach to page layouts.*

Bold colours

When you are mounting photographs of happy children playing with brightly coloured toys or running about on a sunny beach, your backgrounds can be as bold and bright as possible to create an explosion of colour. You can either pick up one of the strong colours in the pictures and use a matching or contrasting tone for the whole setting, or go for a multicoloured effect, using all the colours of the rainbow for a really eye-catching layout.

▲ *The yellow background forming a frame around each of the cut-outs of this car has the effect of making them glow.*

◀ *Children's drawings and paintings, especially their self-portraits, make great additions to your layouts. Cut round both artwork and photographs to create amusing collages, and get them to help you with planning the pages.*

▼ *Here the layout is bold and bright but uses a limited colour palette and achieves a patterned quality by repeating two pictures all round the border. It also promises an irresistible surprise under the central flap.*

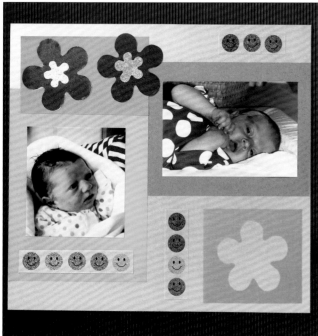

▲ *The two pictures on this layout are very different in character but the colour and black and white have been successfully linked by the shifting tones and consistent shapes of the frames and embellishments.*

▶ *Simple lacing through punched holes creates an eye-catching border for this name tag.*

▼ *This pretty garden of flower babies against a background the colour of a summer sky makes a sweet cover for a family album.*

▲ *This lovely page exhibits the finished results of the bold creative session that is in full swing in the photograph.*

◀ *The simplest shapes cut out of handmade or bark paper and cleverly combined make beautiful original tags and cards.*

▼ *Using a different bright colour for each page of a basic ring bound album turns into it a really striking display that needs no further ornamentation.*

▲ *This digital scrapbook page takes the colour and movement of the sea as its theme, using a section of the photograph itself as part of the background.*

Pale and pastel

Delicately coloured photographs can easily be overwhelmed by a layout that includes strong or dark colours. Softer, paler tones mix and match well with each other and can be used to create a very feminine look, or to give a period setting for a collection of old and perhaps faded prints.

▼ *This pretty floral pattern looks right for the date of the photograph and its colours set off the sepia print perfectly. Toning stripes provide a crisp finishing touch.*

▶ *For a lovely, light-hearted wedding album cover, paste a scattering of tissue paper confetti shapes in mixed pastel colours over a sheet of soft handmade paper.*

Florence

Age 17.

1940

◄ *Pale blue for a boy is enriched by the framing bands of deep blue and the toning pale shades of olive and brown in the background, which carefully echo the soft colours in the photograph.*

◄ *The ice blues of this layout emphasize the coldness of the snow in the photograph. Although the picture was taken in sunny weather there is no colour to warm it up.*

▲ *An enchanting little dog gets her own flowery setting in delicate colours that are just right for her light fur and small size. The daisy chain is threaded with a light touch across the bottom of the page. The simple colour scheme works well.*

▲ *Wearing a pale pink dress, this baby girl is given a traditionally coloured setting on a digitally created page. Touches of warmer pinks add interest to the treatment.*

▶ *The large spots on the girl's clothing were the starting point for this simple design, in which the colours are kept muted and pale so that the picture is the strongest element.*

Shabby chic

Mix-and-match patterns and textures with a confident hand for an eclectic, layered look with a timeless feel. This kind of treatment goes wonderfully with old family photographs and ornate memorabilia, evoking the richness of family history and the way in which possessions are gradually acquired and collected together in a home to make a harmonious whole.

▲ *Handmade papers in soft colours, which can often be found with flower petals or leaves incorporated in their surface, mix beautifully with pressed flowers, ribbons and other scraps to make albums and folders.*

◄ *Scrapbooking websites offer a host of different patterned papers, which can be used for onscreen layouts or downloaded and printed. Ornate historical patterns set off the elaborate dresses of past generations.*

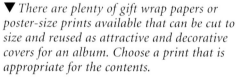

▼ *There are plenty of gift wrap papers or poster-size prints available that can be cut to size and reused as attractive and decorative covers for an album. Choose a print that is appropriate for the contents.*

▲ *Colour-printed die-cut scraps were collected in the 19th century to fill scrapbooks and make decorative collages on items such as trays and screens. Reproductions are now available to add instant Victorian charm to cards and tags.*

▼ *Richly patterned and gilded paper is ideal for embellishments such as envelopes and pouches to hold small treasures. Fasten their flaps with paper or silk flowers to complete the ornate effect.*

▲ *In the 19th century, the sending of greetings cards became extremely popular and many elaborate designs were produced, featuring flowers and hearts, intricate paper lace and ribbons. Their complexity and delicate charm provides inspiration for newly crafted displays in period style.*

▲ *A collage made up of old-fashioned items of ephemera immediately sets the tone for shabby chic. You could use this kind of background as a means of displaying old black-and-white photographs.*

▲ *The exuberant colours of mass-produced Victorian prints and scraps reflect the enthusiasm with which chromolithography, the first system of mass-market colour printing, was greeted when it appeared in the 1830s.*

◄ *Evoke the period of early photography with an abundance of intricate detail in scraps of lace and frills, printed patterns and rich textures. Delicate pressed flowers enhance the faded beauty of old textiles and photographs.*

Journaling

The text you add to your pages adds crucial meaning to the images, filling in all the details you know about when and where the pictures were taken and what was happening at the time, as well as identifying the people featured in them. There are many creative ways to add journaling so that it is not only informative but also becomes an intrinsic and attractive part of the design.

▲ *If you have original letters to accompany your photographs, they can be copied and used as part of your display, or tucked safely into envelopes attached to the pages.*

Victory in Europe
V.E. Day Celebrations

This photo is of my Mum, Nan and Aunty Bar. The huge teapot was probably borrowed from the Street warden who would have used it in the Air Raid Shelter to make Tea during the raids. My Mum was Fifteen years old when the war ended and had been Bombed out of her house twice. There were Ammunition Factories in Ashton so were a major target for enemy Bomber Planes during the war.

My Grandad, pictured here with his friends was still in Europe on V.E. day, his job as a Despatch rider meant he was one of the first people inside the Concentration Camps when the war ended, and witnessed firsthand the horrors that Hitler had inflicted on the Jewish people .

Street party held at Foxcote road, Ashton, Bristol

▲ *In heritage layouts it's often important to explain the historical background to the photographs as well as establishing identities and locations.*

◀ *On this layout for a new baby the words encapsulating the feelings of the proud parents are addressed to the little boy, who will read them in the future.*

▲ *Old-fashioned wax seals and stamps can be purchased at craft stores. They can add the finishing touch to an album page.*

▶ *Instead of providing a commentary on these pictures, the journaling here is a collection of single words conveying the character of the child and all the aspects of a day on the farm.*

▲ Beautifully formed lettering made with a calligraphy pen can become a focal point of a scrapbook design, or as here, the front of an album cover.

▲ Random words forming the background to this sequence of pictures convey ideas associated with the pleasures of travel, while a panel records the details.

My Great-Grandfathers
Fathers of the Bride and Groom

MY GRANDFATHERS

Two old men in sepia
Stand with flowers in hand
At my parents wedding
My god how proud they stand

My Victorian grand-pa-pa's
With shining boots and heads of grey
Caught in a moment from the past
Prepared for the wedding day

If only they could tell us
Of the places they had been
Of mining tales and sailing ships
And places we've never seen

Perhaps a tale of comrades gone
When a great war swept like a flood
To leave young Uncle Tom
In the Gallipoli mud

Of my loved Victorian gents
The memory still remains
What noble lineage are we now
With such blood in our veins

By Bob Dufty

◀ Writing in pen and ink takes time and practice to get right, but gives your work a beautiful hand-crafted, personal quality that cannot be replicated on a computer.

▲ If you have an aptitude for creative writing, an original poem can make a telling contribution. Or you could quote the work of others if the sentiments are appropriate.

Display and presentation

As well as making album pages for your scrapbook, you can also use your presentation skills to mount photographs and other family memorabilia for decorating album covers, memory boxes, memory quilts and even three-dimensional displays.

Archive albums in various formats and bindings are available from scrapbooking stores and other craft suppliers, but you can also buy all the fittings and materials you need to make your own. These unusual formats make particularly attractive gifts commemorating special occasions such as a wedding or the arrival of a baby.

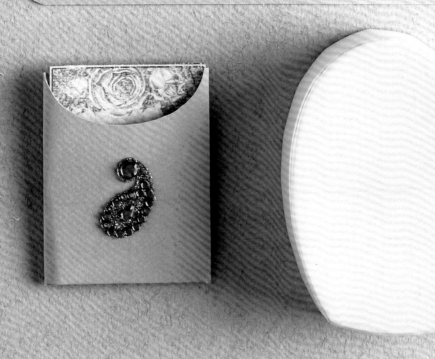

ALBUM COVERS

Designing a special cover for each album gives you a wonderful opportunity to establish its theme and character, so that everyone who sees it will want to look inside and will know instantly what the subject of the chosen album is.

Baby girl album cover

This charming project provides an ideal way to display your favourite baby pictures, and the album will become a family heirloom to be treasured. Make one for each new child in the family, or give them as presents to parents or doting grandparents.

materials and equipment

- metal ruler
- craft knife
- cutting mat
- self-adhesive mount board
- pencil
- polyester wadding (batting), 35 x 33cm/14 x 13in
- scissors
- two pieces of fabric, 35 x 33cm/14 x 13in
- glue stick
- masking tape
- photograph, 15 x 10cm/ 6 x 4in
- watercolour paper, 3 x 30cm/ 1¼ x 12in
- stickers
- hole punch
- 20 sheets of watercolour paper, 29 x 27cm/11¾ x 10¾in
- ribbon

1 Using a metal ruler and craft knife and working on a cutting mat, cut three rectangles each 30 x 28cm/12 x 11¼in and one 30 x 25cm/12 x 10in from self-adhesive mount board. On the smaller rectangle, use a pencil and ruler or set square to draw lines 8cm/3¼in in from each edge to form the aperture for the picture.

2 To make the frame, use a craft knife to cut out the central rectangle and discard. Peel off the protective paper from the adhesive on the mount board and stick the piece of wadding, cut to size, over the frame. Using scissors, trim the wadding to the same size as the mount board.

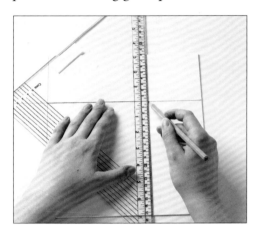

3 Place one rectangle of fabric right side down and lay the frame over it with the wadding underneath. Fold the surplus fabric to the wrong side of the mount board, mitring the corners carefully. Use a glue stick to secure the raw edges to the frame.

4 Cut two diagonal slits in the centre of the fabric, fold the surplus fabric to the back and glue down. Tape the photograph face down over the aperture so that the picture is visible from the padded fabric side. Cover one of the larger rectangles of mount board with the other piece of fabric.

5 Stick the narrow strip of watercolour paper down one long edge of a second large piece of mount board, then stick the frame in place over the rest of the board. Score along the line where the paper and frame join, so that the cover will open flat. Stick the remaining board to the wrong side of the fabric-covered board to form the back cover.

6 Position a coloured sticker at each corner of the photograph at the front of the album to disguise any raw edges of fabric. For extra security for the stickers, dab a tiny spot of glue from a glue stick on to the fabric as well.

7 Punch two holes centrally at the left edge of the front and back covers and the sheets of watercolour paper; the paper will form the album pages. Position the front and back covers on each side of the pages and lace them together with ribbon.

8 Tie the ribbon ends in a bow. Add a few more stickers above and below the bow along the strip of watercolour paper to complete the cover.

Christmas album cover

A pair of square cake boards in a seasonal design, joined together by simple metal screw posts, form the cover of this festive album. A pair of Scottie dogs, cut from sticky-backed felt, complement the plaid design used here and make a charming motif for the front cover. Use this book when planning your Christmas celebrations: there is plenty of room for guest lists, seating plans, special recipes and gift ideas, and after the festivities you can add Christmas memorabilia such as greetings cards and photos.

materials and equipment

- 2 foil cake boards, 25cm/10in square
- double-sided carpet tape
- scissors
- metallic red corrugated cardboard
- self-adhesive felt in green, black and white
- leather hole punch
- 2 screw posts
- black card (stock)
- pencil
- black cotton tape
- tracing paper
- narrow ribbon
- PVA (white) glue
- self-adhesive black cloth tape
- bradawl (awl)
- 4 split pins

1 Place the cake boards side by side, turning them to find the best position to join them (aiming to match the pattern). Stick a 2cm/¾in strip of double-sided carpet tape down each of the edges to be joined.

2 Cut a strip of corrugated cardboard measuring 10 x 25cm/4 x 10in. Stick this over the tape, joining the boards but leaving a 1cm/⅜in gap between them to accommodate the pages.

3 Turn the boards over and cut a rectangle of green self-adhesive felt large enough to cover the inside of the cover. Remove the backing paper and stick in place. Using a leather hole punch, make holes in the top and bottom of the back board, close to the edge of the corrugated cardboard strip. Push a screw post into each hole.

VARIATION: Album cover with a window

Although this album cover has a different subject matter, it is constructed in the same way as the Christmas album cover. The difference is that this album has a window cut in the front, and it has been covered with green felt.

4 From the black card cut 30 sheets 24cm/9½in square and 30 strips 4 × 24cm/ 1½ × 9½in. Make a hole gauge from a spare strip of card and punch out the holes in the card pages and strips. Slip them alternately on to the screw posts.

5 Poke two small holes in the front of the corrugated spine. Thread black tape through the holes and tie in a bow for decoration.

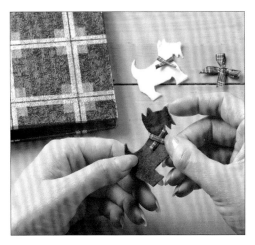

6 Draw a Scottie dog template and use it to cut out a black and a white felt dog. Cross a short length of narrow plaid ribbon at the neck of each dog and glue in position.

7 Remove the backing from each dog. Stick the dogs on to the lower right corner of the front cover, so that the white one slightly overlaps the black one.

8 Cut a rectangle of self-adhesive black felt to make a title plaque. At each corner, push a hole through the cloth, board and green felt using a bradawl. Insert a split pin in each hole and open it up on the inside.

Wedding album cover

The covers of this flamboyant album are made from sturdy silver cake boards, and the front cover is smothered in silk blooms that have been attached to a clear polypropylene sheet. Inside, the album is bound with screw posts, allowing you to add or remove pages as you wish.

1 Using a craft knife and metal ruler on a cutting mat, cut a rectangle of polypropylene measuring 30 × 65cm/12 × 25½in. Score two parallel lines, 5cm/2in apart, across the mid-line, for the spine.

2 Reinforce the spine area on the inside with two lengths of self-adhesive cloth tape, positioning each one centrally over a scored line. Trim the ends flush with the cover.

materials and equipment

- craft knife
- metal ruler
- cutting mat
- polypropylene sheet
- scissors
- self-adhesive cloth tape
- punch
- tack hammer
- assorted silk flowers, large and small
- split pins
- epoxy glue
- 2m/2¼yd wide satin ribbon
- double-sided carpet tape
- 3 silver cake boards, each 30cm/12in square
- weights
- 2 screw posts
- photographic refill pages

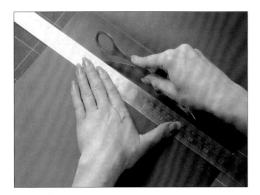

3 Using a punch and hammer, make two holes for the screw posts near the top and bottom of the back cover, in the area reinforced by the cloth tape.

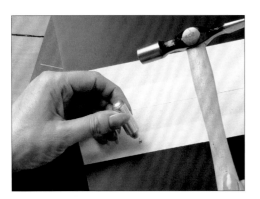

4 Arrange the silk flowers on the front cover and mark the position of the centre of each large flower. Cut the bulbous end from the base of each flower using sturdy scissors. Press a split pin through the hole in the centre of each large flower.

5 Using a craft knife, make a small slit at one of the marks on the cover. (Start in the centre and work outwards.) Put your finger firmly on top of the split pin in a large flower and push the ends through the slit.

6 Open the ends of the split pin at the back. Repeat for the other large flowers. Once they are all in place, fill in any gaps by attaching single petals here and there using epoxy glue.

7 Use epoxy glue to attach smaller silk flowers and petals all around the edge of the cover, so that the plastic is completely hidden by them.

8 Cut a length of ribbon long enough to wrap around the book and tie in a bow. Cut another piece to wrap over the spine. With the cover open, lay the longer piece horizontally across the centre of the spine, then wrap the other piece around the spine. Stick both pieces of ribbon in place using double-sided carpet tape.

9 Punch holes in two of the cake boards to correspond with the holes made in the back cover for the screw posts. Sandwich the polypropylene cover, with the horizontal ribbon attached, between the boards, silver side out, and glue all the layers together. Leave the back boards under a weight until the glue is dry. Glue the front cover to the last cake board, with the ribbon sandwiched between and the silver facing out, so that the board forms the inside of the front cover.

10 Position the board so that a narrow silver border is left all around the edge. Leave the glue to harden with the back cover hanging over a table edge and weight the front cover with small weights. Insert the screw posts through the back cover, slip on the photographic refill pages and screw to secure. Tie the ribbon in a decorative bow to close the album.

Patchwork album cover

You do not need to be a skilled stitcher to accomplish a patchwork cover, as the patches are held securely in place with bonding web before sewing. Follow the patchwork pattern known as "Log Cabin" to arrange fabric strips around a central image or position patchwork squares in a random arrangement.

materials and equipment

- small album
- tape measure
- dressmaker's scissors
- extra-heavy non-woven interfacing
- fusible bonding web
- iron
- photograph printed on fabric using image transfer paper
- cotton print fabric in several colours
- pressing cloth
- sewing machine
- sewing thread
- dressmaker's pins

1 Measure the opened book and add 2cm/¾in to the height and 10cm/4in to the width measurements to allow for hems and side flaps. Following these measurements, cut out a piece of extra-heavy non-woven interfacing and a piece of fusible bonding web. Following the manufacturer's instructions, iron the bonding web to the interfacing. Peel off the backing paper.

2 Position your chosen image transfer so that it will appear centrally on the front cover. For the random arrangement, cut small squares of fabric and arrange them around the photo, overlapping them slightly.

3 When you have covered the front and back completely, place a pressing cloth over the patchwork and iron to fuse the scraps to the interfacing.

4 On a sewing machine, topstitch along all the joins between the patches with a satin stitch to cover the raw edges. Overcast around the the outer edges of the cover. With right sides together, turn in 5cm/2in down each short side and pin in place. Stitch along each end of these turnings with a 1cm/⅜in seam to make the side flaps, then turn right side out. Insert the album.

VARIATIONS: Cloth covers and books

For a fabric album cover, measure the opened book and add 2cm/¾in to the height and width measurements for seam allowances. Cut two flaps from contrasting fabric. Turn in and stitch narrow hems on each flap. Decorate the front cover with appliqué and beads, then pin on the flaps, right sides together, stitch with 1cm/⅜in seams and turn.

A cloth book makes a lovely personalized gift album for a baby, and can be filled with familiar images transferred on to fabric. Cut out double pages from sturdy wool fabric or felt and stitch a picture on each page, using images of special people or animals. Add a favourite motif to the front cover and stitch all the layers together at the spine.

ACCORDION ALBUMS

This ingenious and flexible format allows you to protect precious photographs and documents inside an album that closes between hard covers like a book, but can also be fully opened out to make a free-standing display on a table or mantelpiece.

Concertina book

Make this pretty accordion album to hold some of your favourite themed photographs. Choose a selection of luxurious decorative papers in similar shades of mauve for a really striking effect.

materials and equipment

- large rubber stamp in a leaf motif
- metallic ink stamp pad
- translucent paper
- craft knife
- metal ruler
- cutting mat
- thick cardboard
- decorative metallic paper
- glue stick
- bone folder
- handmade paper

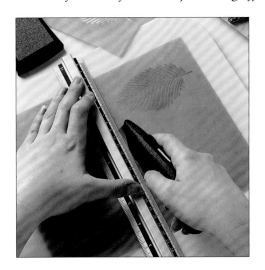

1 Stamp the motif on to a selection of papers to choose the effects you like best. To do this, press the stamp into the ink pad to coat the surface with ink, then press the stamp on the paper. Lift it up carefully to avoid smudging. In this case, the motif was stamped on translucent paper using metallic ink. Take care when stamping on to tracing paper, as some stamping inks do not dry well on the resistant surface. If you have difficulty, stamp on a lightweight handmade paper instead. Cut out the motif using a craft knife and metal ruler and working on a cutting mat.

2 To make the front and back covers of the album, cut two pieces of thick cardboard to the required size using a craft knife and metal ruler, and working on a cutting mat. Then cut two pieces of decorative metallic paper 2.5cm/1in larger all round than the cardboard. Lay the paper right side down and glue one piece of cardboard to the centre of each piece. Cut across the corners of the paper, then glue the edges and carefully fold them over to stick them down securely on the cardboard. Turn the front cover over and glue the stamped leaf motif in the centre.

◀**3** Cut a long strip of translucent paper slightly narrower than the height of the cover boards. This will form the folded pages of the album. Measure the width of the album cover and make folds along the strip of paper to match. To do this, carefully and accurately measure the distance from one fold to another; use a metal ruler and bone folder to score and crease the paper to produce a succession of accordion folds. Trim off any excess paper at the end. When you have finished, ensure that the paper folds into a neat pile, and that it fits neatly inside the album.

4 Glue one end of the folded translucent paper on to the front cover of the album, then cover the whole with a sheet of handmade paper to coordinate with the rest of the album. Stick the other end of the translucent paper to the back cover and cover this with a second sheet of handmade paper. Fold up the book and place it under a heavy weight to prevent the papers from buckling as the glue dries.

Accordion wrap

This attractive book uses a folding technique developed in Japan to store long scrolls of paper. The paper used here for the covers contains fragments of coloured silk and threads, added to the paper pulp before forming the sheets.

materials and equipment

- 2 pieces of mounting board, 15 x 20cm/6 x 8in
- glue stick
- 2 sheets of handmade paper, 19 x 24cm/7½ x 9½in
- scissors
- craft knife
- metal ruler
- cutting mat
- narrow satin ribbon
- tapestry needle
- white cartridge (construction) paper 112 x 19cm/44 x 7½in
- bone folder

1 To make the covers, apply glue to one side of each piece of mounting board. Place the board centrally on the wrong side of each piece of handmade paper.

2 Cut diagonally across the corners of the two sheets of paper. Fold the excess paper over the boards and glue in place.

3 Using a craft knife, metal ruler and cutting mat, cut a 1cm/⅜in slit in the centre of each long side on both covers.

4 Cut four 25cm/10in lengths of ribbon. Using a tapestry needle, thread one through each slit and glue the end to the board.

5 Using the bone folder, fold the cartridge paper into accordion pleats to form eight equal sections using accordion pleats.

6 Glue the end sections of the paper to the inside of the covers, positioning them centrally. Make sure the two covers line up.

7 Tie one pair of ribbons to create a book with turning pages.

VARIATION: Fan book

Fold a circle of paper into twelfths and cut down one fold to the centre. Trim the edge. Make two covers to fit the shape and glue to the end folds.

DISPLAY BOARDS

Rather than keeping all your creative ideas tucked away in albums, it can be fun to make scrapbook-style displays to go on the wall. Old prints fade easily, so it is a good idea to have copies made to use in this way and to keep the originals safely away from the light.

Seaside memory board

This collection of holiday memories serves both as a decorative feature for your wall and as a noticeboard to which other mementoes can be added from time to time. It could even be used as a memo board for day-to-day reminders. While you are on your trip, persuade the whole family to look for pretty souvenirs to remind them of your happy time on the beach together.

materials and equipment

- collection of seaside photographs
- pictures from printed sources of marine subjects such as sea, sand, sky, pebbles and shells
- old maps showing large areas of sea
- natural objects such as feathers and small shells
- scissors
- metal ruler
- craft knife
- cutting mat
- lightweight white board
- textured paper
- spray adhesive
- transparent photo corners

1 Spread out your family photographs, together with printed pictures from other sources, maps and seaside ephemera, to decide which to use. Cut out some of the background material with scissors, tear some pictures to give them ragged edges, and trim others with a metal ruler and craft knife so that you have a range of different textures and edges to the collection.

2 Assemble the larger, more abstract pictures of sky and sea on the board, overlapping them with areas of textured paper to make a background for the photographs. When you are happy with the arrangement, glue the background pictures down securely with spray adhesive. Arrange feathers and other pieces of seaside ephemera on the board.

◀ **3** Complete the memory board by adding your photographs to the arrangement, and secure them using transparent photo corners. If you are using duplicate prints you could stick them in position with glue once you have finalized the composition, but using photo corners enables you to place other mementoes behind the photos as your collection grows. Glue additional pieces of ephemera, such as small shells, around the photographs.

VARIATION: Seashore album

For a seaside-themed album, cover the boards with an enlarged detail of a photograph of sand and sea, and glue a real seashell to the front – look for flat shells when you're on the beach.

Pressed flower noticeboard

Natural linen and linen tape tone beautifully with the pressed flowers and leaves and the colour-washed wooden frame in this attractive design.

materials and equipment

- large, flat, rectangular wooden picture frame
- off-white emulsion (latex) paint
- medium-sized decorator's paintbrush
- pressed flowers and leaves
- measuring tape
- PVA (white) glue
- fine artist's paintbrush
- spray matt acrylic varnish
- natural linen or linen-look fabric
- scissors
- sheet of MDF (medium density fibreboard) cut to fit frame
- staple gun
- soft pencil
- linen dressmaking tape
- hammer
- decorative upholstery nails
- picture wire or cord for hanging

1 Paint the picture frame with a coat of off-white emulsion (latex) paint. Apply the paint in a thin wash, so that the texture of the wood shows through. Leave to dry.

2 Arrange the flowers and leaves with the help of a measuring tape. Starting in the centre of one short side of the frame and working outwards, apply a little PVA glue to the back of each flower and stick in place.

3 When the design is complete, leave until the glue is dry then spray the frame with matt acrylic varnish. Repeat if necessary but take care not to flatten the flowers.

4 Cut a piece of linen 5cm/2in larger all round than the MDF. Stretch the fabric over the board and secure it at the back with a staple gun, starting in the centre of each side and folding the corners neatly.

5 On the right side, mark out a large central diamond using a soft pencil. Cut four lengths of linen tape to fit and lay in place, stapling them together at the corners.

6 Arrange more lines of tape in a pleasing design, weaving them over and under each other. Trim the ends and secure at the back of the board with the staple gun.

7 On the right side, secure the linen tape with upholstery nails spaced at regular intervals. Fit the decorated board into the frame and attach picture wire or cord.

HERITAGE QUILTS

Traditional quilts have often been used to record special events or memories by applying embroidery or incorporating symbolic patchwork shapes. With the latest range of transfer papers you can now create a photographic quilt made up of family pictures for posterity too.

Memory quilt

This beautiful album quilt was made to commemorate the 70th birthday of the maker's mother. Some of the ivory silk fabric used was taken from a wedding dress, giving it particular sentimental value.

materials and equipment

- black and white photographs
- scraps of ivory silk in a variety of textures and shades
- image transfer paper
- iron
- paper
- pencil
- dressmaker's scissors
- calico
- measuring tape
- dressmaker's pins
- sewing machine
- ivory sewing thread
- ivory silk for the quilt backing
- quilt interlining
- tacking thread and needle
- coffee silk for binding the edges
- metallic sewing thread

1 Transfer the photographs on to silk, using a transfer paper suitable for the fabric. Decide on the finished block size and estimate how many blocks you will need to make by working out a plan on paper. Cut the block squares from calico, adding a seam allowance all around of 2cm/¾in. Trim each transferred photograph and pin to the block through the border to avoid damaging the prints.

2 Cut random strips of different silks. Pin one strip right side down to one side of the photograph. Stitch the strip down, making sure the seam does not obscure the image, then flip the strip over to conceal the stitching and press lightly. Add the next strip at an angle, covering the end of the previous strip. Repeat, working clockwise round the image, and cut away excess fabric from each strip before adding the next.

3 Complete each calico block in the same way, mixing the colours and textures of silk randomly. When you have added all the strips, press each patch then trim away the excess fabric with scissors, leaving a 2cm/¾in seam allowance around the block.

4 Pin and stitch the blocks together in rows, adding extra strips of silk between them. Join the rows, then add a border. To assemble the quilt, place the backing right side down and the interlining on top. Finally place the quilt top right side up on top. Tack (baste) all three layers together.

5 Decorate the quilt with machine or hand quilting before binding the edges with coffee silk. Finish the design with machine embroidery using metallic thread in a zig-zag or other embroidery stitch.

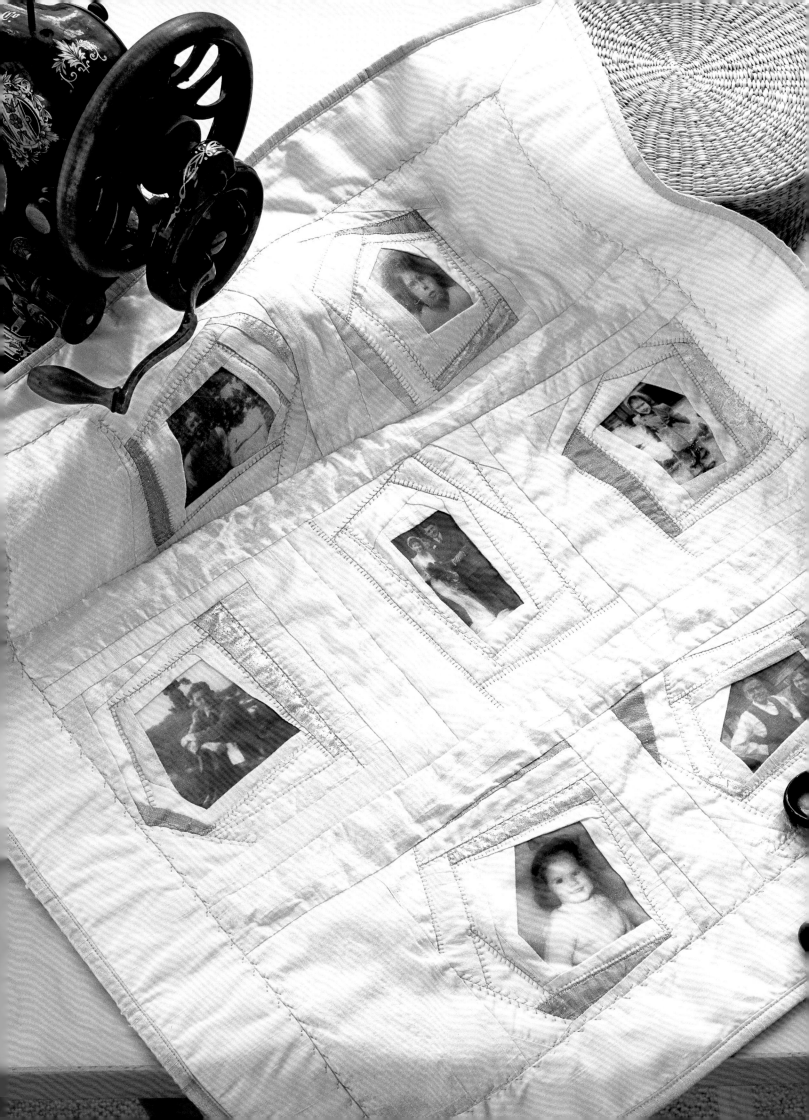

Paper quilt wallhanging

In this exciting and original hanging, the images are not just framed but actually become part of the vibrantly coloured handmade paper squares. Paper pulp and pigments for dyeing it can be bought from craft suppliers.

materials and equipment

- collection of photographs or other souvenirs such as tickets, labels or press cuttings
- aluminium mesh
- strong scissors
- 2.5cm/1in-wide masking tape
- absorbent non-woven kitchen cloths
- recycled paper pulp
- paper dyes in 2–3 colours
- 2–3 large plastic bowls
- paper string or embroidery thread (floss)
- 60cm/24in dowelling, 6mm/¼in diameter

1 With your collection of materials in front of you, decide on a standard size for each patch and the number of patches that are required to make the hanging. In this case each patch will be 15cm/6in square.

2 To make the moulds for the paper, cut a 17.5cm/7in square of aluminium mesh, and a strip 15 × 4cm/6 × 1½in. Fold strips of masking tape over each edge of the mesh shapes to cover the sharp edges.

3 Cover a large board with several layers of non-woven kitchen cloth. Dye two or three batches of pulp following the manufacturer's instructions. Immerse the square mesh in the background colour pulp and lift the first square out of the bowl.

4 Turn the mesh carefully to deposit the square in the top corner of the couching cloth. Repeat to make a total of nine squares, laying them in three rows of three. Use the masking tape binding as a guide for the spacing between the squares.

5 Cut 36 lengths of paper string or embroidery thread 10cm/4in long, and lay them over the spaces to join the squares. Cut nine lengths 9cm/3½in long to make the hanging loops. Double these and arrange them along one side.

6 Couch nine more squares of the same coloured pulp on top of the first set, to hold the strings or threads in place.

7 Arrange your collection of images centrally on the squares of wet pulp.

8 Using different coloured pulp and the smaller mould, couch strips of pulp over the edges of the images to hold them in place. Leave for several days to dry naturally, then thread the dowelling rod through the loops.

KEEPSAKE BOXES

For small collections, or treasured three-dimensional objects that cannot be fitted into an album, a keepsake box is the answer. Look out for good quality packaging that can be recycled, or buy plain cardboard boxes from craft stores and decorate them to match the subject of your collection.

Découpage memory box

The art of decorating with paper scraps, which are overlaid and varnished to give the appearance of a hand-painted finish is known as découpage. This box is prettily decorated with pictures of coloured feathers, cats, flowers and fans, and finished with a pink ribbon border – every girl's ideal treasure box.

materials and equipment

- plain hexagonal cardboard box with lid
- acrylic or household emulsion (latex) paint in eau de Nil
- paintbrush
- scraps of old manuscript paper, or new paper aged by dyeing in tea
- glue stick
- selection of cut-out paper scraps printed with images of cats, fans, feathers and flowers
- acrylic matt varnish
- measuring tape
- scissors
- fabric ribbon
- fabric glue
- assorted buttons
- needle and thread

1 Paint the box inside and out with two coats of eau de Nil paint and leave to dry. Tear the manuscript paper into scraps and glue these to the sides and lid of the box. Cover with the printed scraps, overlapping them as desired. Apply two to three coats of acrylic varnish, leaving each coat to dry.

2 Measure the rim of the lid and cut a length of ribbon to this measurement. Using fabric glue, stick the ribbon around the rim. Using the same glue, stick a selection of buttons in assorted designs around the rim, on top of the ribbon.

3 Make a simple rosette shape with another length of ribbon and secure by stitching through the central folds. Stitch a button in to the centre, then glue the rosette to the centre of the box lid.

VARIATION: Travel memory box

To house a collection of holiday souvenirs, cover a travel-themed memory box with découpage using scraps of maps featuring appropriate destinations.

Fabric-covered box

Covering a box with a luxurious fabric such as linen, velvet or silk makes a very special setting for small treasures such as a collection of love letters and romantic trinkets. This box is cleverly constructed with ribbon ties so that it lies flat before assembly and could make a lovely surprise gift. If you are making the box as a memento of a family wedding you may even be able to obtain a little spare wedding dress fabric to make an extra-special reminder of the occasion for the bride.

materials and equipment

- craft knife
- metal ruler
- cutting mat
- strong cardboard
- squared pattern paper
- pencil
- scissors
- dressmaker's pins
- pale lilac linen
- dressmaker's scissors
- tacking (basting) thread
- needle
- narrow velvet ribbon
- grosgrain ribbon
- Ric-rac braid
- sewing machine
- sewing thread
- iron
- small embroidered motif
- fabric glue

1 Using a craft knife and metal ruler and working on a cutting mat, from strong cardboard cut out a base and a lid, each 19 × 15cm/7½ × 6in; two long sides each 19 × 7.5cm/7½ × 3in; and two short sides each 15 × 7.5cm/6 × 3in. These will be slipped inside the cover to make the box rigid.

2 Make a paper pattern using the measurements on the template at the back of the book as a guide. Add a 1.5cm/⅝in seam allowance all around the pattern. Pin the pattern to a piece of lilac linen folded in half along the grain and cut out two matching pieces of fabric.

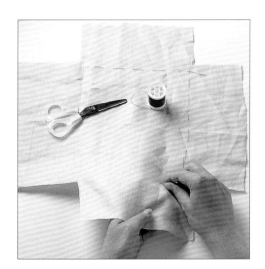

3 Using a contrasting coloured thread, and working on the piece of fabric intended for the right side of the cover, tack (baste) the fabric to mark out the stitching lines for the different sections of the box, following the guides on the template. Cut eight 15cm/6in lengths of narrow velvet ribbon for the corner ties and two 30cm/12in lengths of grosgrain ribbon for the front ties.

VARIATIONS: More fabric ideas

To memorialize a beloved pet, cover a box with fabric on to which you have transferred a favourite photograph.

Cover an old shoe box with decorative papers or fabrics appropriate for the occasion and add ribbons.

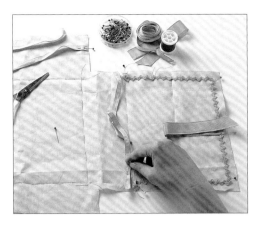

4 On the right side of the fabric, pin and tack a length of Ric-rac braid along the seam line around three sides of the box lid. Pin the ties in place at the corners and pin one piece of grosgrain ribbon to the lid.

5 Pin the last piece of grosgrain ribbon to the centre front section of the box base. Stitch the ribbon ties down with a straight machine stitch, turning the raw edges underneath to neaten.

6 Pin the two pieces of fabric right sides together and stitch all around the edges of the box. Leave the long side at the front of the base open so that the cardboard sections can be slipped inside the cover. Clip the corners and trim the seam allowance, then turn the cover through to the right side and press.

7 Push the first piece of cardboard for the lid through the opening along the long side. Neatly stitch along the lid edge to enclose it using a zipper foot on the machine. Insert the cardboard for the long side at the back and enclose with another line of stitches, followed by the pieces for the short sides and the large piece for the base. Enclose each piece of cardboard with a line of stitches. Finally, insert the last piece for the long side at the front of the box.

8 When all the cardboard is in place, turn in the seam allowance of the opening and neatly slipstitch the seam. Glue an embroidered motif on to the box lid with fabric glue. Then tie the ribbon ties at each corner to assemble the box.

THREE-DIMENSIONS

The crafts of paper folding and paper sculpture open up many new avenues for creativity in scrapbooking. Here are two very simple ideas to start you thinking in three dimensions when devising themed settings for your photographs.

Our house

This fold-out display is an ideal showcase for photographs of a house renovation. Remember to preserve a piece of that ghastly old wallpaper that took you hours of work to remove.

materials and equipment

- three sheets of white cartridge (construction) paper, two measuring 38 x 60cm/15 x 24in and one 19 x 30cm/7½ x 12in
- bone folder
- pencil
- metal ruler
- craft knife
- cutting mat
- glue stick
- bulldog clips

1 To make the accordion-style house on the right of the design, fold the small sheet of paper in half lengthwise, then fold the long ends back to align with the centre fold. Crease the folds sharply using a bone folder. Open the paper out, then fold it in half widthwise. Open out the sheet and mark in the pointed roofs on the two centre sections, following the template at the back of the book. Using a craft knife and a metal ruler and working on a cutting mat, cut out the roof sections and cut out two small windows under each pointed roof. Fold the design widthwise and glue the two sides of each outer section together so that the house will stand up.

2 To make the folded house at the left of the design, take a large sheet of paper and fold over a third of it at the right-hand side. On this third, lightly draw a pointed roof and windows. Cut out the roof and windows as before.

3 For the background, fold in 2cm/¾in down one short side of the last sheet of white paper. Crease the fold sharply using the bone folder. Glue the plain section of the larger house to this flap so that the house can be lifted and turned like the page of a book.

4 Glue one side of the smaller house to the right-hand side of the main album page. Secure the paper with bulldog clips while the glue dries. Arrange photographs and memorabilia on the background page and inside the left-hand house.

Butterfly bonanza

These two charming ideas for presenting a single photograph use matching butterfly motifs, which are folded and glued so that they appear to flutter around the picture. Punched holes give their wings a lacy appearance.

materials and equipment

- pencil
- paper
- scissors
- selection of pastel-coloured papers, including white
- cutting mat
- craft knife
- revolving leather punch
- fancy-edged scissors
- fine corrugated white cardboard
- glue stick
- heavy white paper
- coloured card (stock)
- photographs
- transparent photo corners

1 Enlarge the butterfly template at the back of the book in three different sizes and cut them out. Place a template on a piece of folded coloured paper and trace around it. Cut out the small angled shapes in the wings using a craft knife and working on a cutting mat, and make decorative round holes in various sizes using a leather punch.

2 Keeping the paper folded, cut round the outline of the butterfly with fancy-edged scissors. Make a selection of butterfly motifs in different sizes and colours. Do not flatten out the central folds. To make winged cards, cut out one wing only, then cut out a rectangle around the wing using fancy-edged scissors. Fold the wing outwards.

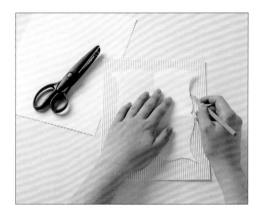

3 To make a foundation on which to mount the butterflies, enlarge the frame template so that it is about 2.5cm/1in larger all round than the photograph, then cut it out. Position it on a piece of white corrugated cardboard and draw round it lightly with a pencil. Cut out the shape, taking care not to crush the ridges of the cardboard. Glue the cut-out on to a slightly larger rectangle of heavy white paper and mount this on a larger piece of coloured card.

VARIATION: Butterfly theme

Butterflies are a perennially popular motif. They can be stencilled, stamped, cut out from paper and applied in different ways to album pages.

4 Carefully make four tiny marks at the corners where you intend to mount the photograph, then arrange the butterfly motifs around the frame, slotting some individual butterflies inside the winged cards. Glue them in place using a glue stick. Finally, attach the photograph to the mount using transparent photo corners.

5 To make the photo mailer, cut a long strip of heavy white paper slightly wider than the photograph and long enough to enclose it plus an overlap for the butterfly. Crease the vertical folds. Cut out one small and one large butterfly motif from coloured paper, then cut out a half large motif from the end flap. Using the photo as a guide, position and cut four diagonal slots to take the corners.

6 Assemble the photo mailer by sticking the large butterfly to the front of the card in such a position that the wings slot through the folded half motif cut in the flap. The action of slotting the wings together will keep the card closed. Stick a small motif on the front of the card and mount the photograph inside.

Children

Babies and children are of course among the most popular subjects for scrapbooking: all parents long to preserve their memories of their offspring as they grow up so quickly. For most people, it's also when they have their own children that they become most aware of the need to pass on the family history to future generations. There is nothing older children like more than revisiting their own earliest memories – seeing pictures of their former little selves and being reminded of special times they can just remember, or discovering what they were like as babies, before their memories begin. As well as photographs, of which you will have plenty to choose from, include some of the children's early works of art or attempts at writing.

Album page for a baby boy

Soft pastel shades dictate the look of this album page, which has a contemporary style. Keep a tiny but important memento, such as the baby's hospital identification tag, safely inside a small clear plastic envelope.

1 Cut out rectangles of plain and printed paper, and arrange them on the heavy white paper. Use different-sized rectangles to make a pleasing layout. Glue in position. Arrange the collage items on the background. Small mementoes can be placed in clear plastic envelopes. Glue all the background items in place.

2 Take a small piece of white card and draw a simple motif, such as a toy boat, on the wrong side of it. Working on a cork mat or corrugated cardboard to protect the work surface, use a bodkin or paper piercer to make pinpricks at regular intervals along the outline of the design using the pencil line as a guide.

materials and equipment

- scissors
- plain paper in pastel colours
- striped printed paper, such as wallpaper
- heavy white paper
- glue stick
- baby mementoes
- small, clear plastic envelope
- white card (stock)
- pencil
- cork mat or corrugated cardboard
- bodkin or paper piercer
- fancy-edged scissors in wavy and postage stamp designs
- rotating leather hole punch
- lettering stencil
- craft knife
- cutting mat
- baby Ric-rac braid

3 Cut out a rectangle of blue paper using wavy-edged scissors. Then cut out the pinpricked motif with fancy-edged scissors in a postage stamp design and glue it on the blue paper.

VARIATION: A patchwork background

Simple photographs can be enhanced in many ways. Here a single photograph takes centre stage and the ephemera that is added is colour co-ordinated to hold the design idea together. The stripey pastel patchwork background is appropriately coloured for a baby boy and matches his clothing.

The zipper pocket at the bottom of the page is a good place to keep any small items of memorabilia, such as small cards expressing good wishes from friends and family. The cute faces are a fun addition to this light-hearted album page.

4 Make a mount for the photograph by cutting out a piece of white card larger all round than the photograph, using wavy-edged scissors. Pierce small decorative holes all around the edges of the card using a rotating leather hole punch.

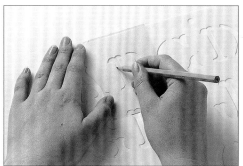

5 Place a lettering stencil over a rectangular piece of blue paper and stencil the letter of your choice on the card. Cut the letter out carefully with a craft knife, working on a cutting mat. Trim the corners of the paper shape with scissors to round them gently.

6 Mount the cut-out letter on a rectangle of pale yellow paper, then on a larger fancy-edged rectangle of white card. Pierce a small hole in the centre top of the label and thread it with a short length of baby Ric-rac braid. Tie this in a bow. Carefully glue everything to the background.

Album page for a baby girl

Pages dedicated to baby girls don't always have to be pale pink and frilly. This cheeky picture called for a bolder treatment, so the page uses bright colours and a stitched paisley motif with the sparkle of tiny gems.

materials and equipment

- scraps of card (card stock)
- pencil
- felt squares in blue, lime green, light purple and dark purple
- scissors
- stranded embroidery thread (floss) in lime green, fuchsia and turquoise
- needle
- small self-adhesive gems
- tweezers
- 30cm/12in square sheet of bright pink card (card stock)
- glue stick
- small buckle
- self-adhesive foam pads
- photograph
- chipboard letters
- craft paint in purple
- artist's brush

1 Draw three large and two small paisley shapes on card and cut them out. Use them as templates to cut out five felt shapes in assorted colours.

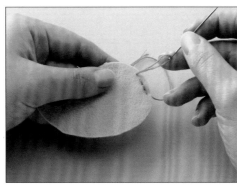

2 Work a row of backstitch around the edge of each felt shape using six strands of contrasting embroidery thread. Work three lazy daisy stitches in the centre of each large shape and one on each small shape.

3 Stick a small self-adhesive gem to the embroidery stitches in the centre of each paisley shape, grasping the gems with tweezers to make this easier.

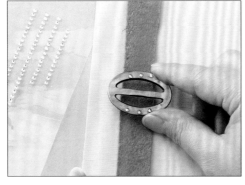

4 Cut a strip of purple felt 2cm/¾in wide and 30cm/12in long and glue it down the left side of the background card near the edge. Decorate a small buckle with more sticky gems and glue it to the felt belt.

5 Glue the decorated felt shapes to the matching card shapes. Stick two foam pads on the back of each small paisley shape so that they will be slightly raised.

6 Position the photograph centrally in the area to the right of the felt strip and glue it to the background. Arrange the three large paisley shapes down the left side of the picture, then position the small shapes between them. Glue all the shapes in place.

7 Paint chipboard letters to spell the child's name in purple to match the felt shapes and leave to dry. Glue them in place at the bottom right of the layout.

{Lilly}

Schoolday memories

This memento of your schooldays will bring back memories of past escapades, glories and disasters. Indulge yourself and relive all those carefree times by making a schooldays album page.

materials and equipment

- brick-effect dolls' house paper
- sharp scissors
- glue stick
- envelope
- selection of school photographs
- transparent photo corners
- small labels
- black pen
- striped grosgrain ribbon
- metal badge
- embroidered pocket and cap badges
- school reports
- star stickers

1 Cut two sheets of brick-effect paper to match the size of your album pages and glue in position. Glue the envelope in one corner so that the flap faces upwards. Arrange the photographs on the page then secure with photo corners.

2 Next to each photograph, stick a handwritten label giving the year each picture was taken (or use computer-printed labels if you prefer). The album pages here show three generations of schoolchildren.

STARTING SCHOOL

Starting school is a major milestone for every child, but after just a few weeks they all seem to settle into their new life, making friends, learning new skills and starting on the path to independence. Mark the progress from the first uncertain day to being one of a trio of best friends with a special album page.

materials and equipment

- 30cm/12in square sheet of plain background paper
- brick-effect paper
- two or more photographs
- photo corners
- small labels
- alphabet fridge magnets
- photocopier
- scissors
- coloured pencils

3 Fold the grosgrain ribbon in half and attach the metal badge to the top of the ribbon near the fold. Trim the ribbon ends to create a V shape. Glue the ribbon to the flap of the envelope. (Always keep a sheet of paper between the two album pages when they are closed to prevent the badge damaging the pictures.)

1 Cut two 2.5cm/1in strips of brick-effect paper and stick them along the top and bottom of the background paper. Mount the photographs in the centre with photo corners. Add a printed or handwritten date label under each.

2 Photocopy the fridge magnets and the pencils, reducing the size as necessary. Cut them out individually and arrange around the pictures. The letters can spell out a caption or be placed randomly. Glue everything in place.

4 Glue the embroidered badges to the pages, positioning the cap badge just above the envelope. Fill the envelope with extra pictures and school reports. Finally, arrange a sprinkling of star stickers over the pages.

Polka-dot mini-album

This handy-sized accordion album, in its own brightly decorated matching box, could be filled with a selection of photographs from every stage of a child's life, to make an enchanting gift for a proud grandparent.

materials and equipment

- rectangular cardboard box
- handmade paper in orange, pink, turquoise and green
- small coins
- pencil
- scissors
- hole punch
- glue stick
- thick card (stock)
- metal ruler
- craft knife and cutting mat
- paper parcel tape
- thin green card
- pair of compasses
- thin satin ribbon

1 Cover the box with orange handmade paper. Draw around small coins on to orange, pink, turquoise and green paper. Cut out all the circles. Punch small holes in the centre of some circles using a hole punch. Glue the circles to the top and sides of the box, overlapping some of them.

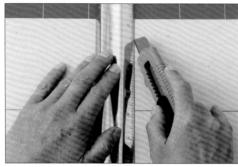

2 Measure and mark out four identical rectangles of thick card to a size that will fit neatly inside the box. Cut them out using a craft knife and a metal ruler and working on a cutting mat.

3 Place the rectangles side by side in a row, leaving gaps of about 3mm/⅛in between them. Cut six strips of paper tape, slightly longer than the card. Stick the tape to the cards, over the gaps, to join them together. Repeat on the other side. Leave to dry, then trim away the excess tape.

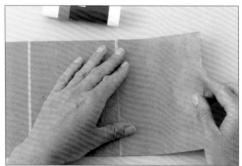

4 Fold along the joins to make an accordion album. Cut eight pieces of turquoise handmade paper to the same dimensions as the cards. Glue one piece to the front and one to the back of each page of the album.

5 Cut six strips of orange paper 2.5cm/1in wide to match the height of the pages. Glue a strip over the middle of each fold on the front and back.

6 Decorate the front of the album with small multicoloured circles of paper to match the box.

7 Draw a circle 6cm/2¼in in diameter on thin green card and cut it out. Trim a small photo into a slightly smaller circle and glue it to the green circle to make a tag.

8 Punch a hole in the top of the tag and add a length of thin satin ribbon as a tie. Fill the album with photographs. Tie the tag around the album to keep it closed, then place the album in the box.

VARIATION: Snow scene

Children playing in the snow are always full of fun and vitality, with bright smiles and rosy cheeks. Once the snow stops falling and the sun comes out, it's a great time to take photographs of them for your album, to store up memories of exciting days.

On this scrapbook page, blue and white spotted paper has been used to resemble a snowy sky, and the torn white edges and glittering stars, plus the pale colouring of all the elements, help to reinforce the cold, bright winter light in the photograph. You could create a similar snowy background for a winter page by sticking on individual self-adhesive dots in a random arrangement on plain paper.

Growing up together

Birthdays, Christmas and Easter holidays are family times that are especially important to grandparents, aunts, uncles and cousins. Keep a record of how the children are growing in the intervening months by collecting together pictures taken on these special occasions.

materials and equipment

- six photographs
- coloured paper
- corner punch
- 30cm/12in square of background paper
- tear-off calendar
- glue stick

1 Trim all the photographs to measure 7 × 9cm/2¾ × 3½in. Glue each on to a piece of coloured paper and trim the margins to 1cm/⅜in all around.

2 Trim the corners with a decorative punch to give the frames a pretty, lacy look.

VARIATION: **Family secrets**

Here's another idea for a family album page that shows all the children together yet allows each of them to make a personal contribution – if you can persuade them to take part.

Create matching mini-folders from thin card (stock), one for each child, and decorate the fronts with small photographs, each mounted on a torn square of handmade floral paper. Fasten each folder with a short loop of ribbon and a small button.

Inside the little folders you could insert a few folded pages of white paper and get each child to write something about themselves and what they have been doing, or make up a story or a poem, or draw some pictures. Alternatively, you could paste in more photographs or other memorabilia, or write your own account of your children's progress and achievements. Decorate the rest of the page with a few small embellishments and give it a title and a date.

You could make a page of this kind every year as an ongoing record of your growing offspring, with pictures shot specially for the album page. Both you and other family members, and the children themselves, will enjoy looking back over the years to see these snapshots of themselves as developing individuals within a family group.

3 Arrange the pictures in two scattered rows of three, in chronological order, on the background paper.

4 Add a few tear-off pages from the calendar, scattered over the page. Circle the dates when the pictures were taken on the calendar pages.

Special occasions

Many of our most memorable and enjoyable experiences occur on the important annual festivals such as Christmas, Easter and Thanksgiving, which give a regular rhythm to family life and are traditionally times when everyone wants to get together with relatives and friends for informal and joyful celebrations.

As well as these parties, there are the very special occasions that mark life's milestones, such as graduation, engagement, marriage and the birth of a baby, to name but a few. All these high days and holidays demand to be commemorated by special pages in your albums, and all make great themes for which a wealth of decorative material is available, as well as a good collection of photographs of the event. The following pages include ideas for pages based on both seasonal festivities and more personal celebrations.

Valentine's celebration

The traditional imagery of Valentine's Day is perfect for an album page expressing the way you feel about your partner. Use the phrases on this layout as inspiration for your own special messages to the one you love.

1 Cut a 12 × 4in/30 × 10cm rectangle of pearl white paper and glue it to the left-hand side of the red card background, aligning the edges, to make a wide border.

2 Print out all the words and phrases, except "Forever", on to white paper. Trim "I love you because…" and "…you're wonderful!" to thin white strips measuring 10 × 2cm/4 × ¾in. Glue to the top and bottom of the border.

3 Glue two swing tags on to the back of a sheet of silver paper, and one on to red paper. Cut the papers to shape by cutting around the edges of the tags. Re-punch the holes with an eyelet punch.

4 Cut out the three printed phrases and glue one to the front of each tag. Punch three small hearts from red vellum and glue these to the tags, over the text.

5 Position the tags on the border. Mark the positions of the holes for the elastic at the sides of the tags and punch the holes with an eyelet punch. Thread the elastic to make crosses and tie at the back. Insert the tags with the red tag in the centre.

6 To make the frame, draw a 12.5 × 15cm/ 5 × 6in rectangle on thick card. Draw a second rectangle inside it, 2cm/¾in smaller all round. Cut it out using a craft knife and metal ruler. Dry-brush a thin coat of parchment-coloured paint over the frame and leave it to dry.

7 Cut out four small discs of white card. Inscribe the letters L, O, V and E on the discs using rub-on letters.

8 Punch a small hole in the top of each disc using an eyelet punch. Insert an eyelet into each, then a length of ribbon. Glue the four discs to the top of the page.

9 Cut out the printed words "you" and "me". Glue them to small heart-shaped tags. Attach the hearts to the page beside the border panel using white eyelets.

materials and equipment

- scissors
- pearl white paper
- metal ruler
- pencil
- craft knife
- cutting mat
- 30cm/12in square sheet of thin red card (stock)
- spray adhesive
- computer and printer
- thin white paper
- 3 small swing tags
- silver and red paper
- small eyelet punch
- tack hammer
- red vellum paper
- heart punch
- thin round elastic in silver
- thick card (stock)
- acrylic paint in parchment
- paintbrush
- white card
- gold rub-on letters
- 6 eyelets
- thin red and silver ribbon
- 2 small heart tags
- white vellum
- thin steel wire
- strong clear glue
- photograph
- masking tape
- 4 photo corners

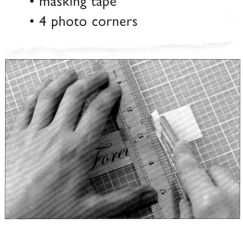

10 Print the word "Forever" on to a sheet of white vellum. Trim closely, then glue with spray adhesive to a larger strip of white vellum. Attach the strip to the bottom of the page.

11 Cut two pieces of steel wire 15cm/6in long. Bend into two hearts. Twist the ends of one heart together and loop the second heart through the first before twisting the ends. Glue the entwined hearts over the vellum panel using strong clear glue.

12 Attach the photo to the back of the painted frame with strips of masking tape. Position the framed picture in the centre of the red area of the page and attach it using photo corners.

An engagement

This simple and beautiful layout expresses a single idea very clearly: the love and happiness of the newly engaged couple. The use of translucent vellum for the heart shapes creates a pretty, layered look. It's essential to use spray adhesive for the vellum, as any other glue will show through.

materials and equipment

- polka-dot paper
- metal ruler
- pencil
- craft knife
- cutting mat
- 30cm/12in square sheet of thin cream card (card stock)
- spray adhesive
- gold paper
- scallop-edged scissors
- red vellum
- light pink vellum
- dark pink paper
- 1 large photograph and 3 small ones

1 Cut a 30 x 18cm/12 x 7in rectangle of polka-dot paper using a craft knife and metal ruler and working on a cutting mat. Glue the paper to the right-hand side of the cream card, aligning the outer edges.

2 Cut three rectangles of gold paper 7 x 5cm/2¾ x 2in, and one 17 x 14.5cm/6¾ x 5¾in. Trim all the sides with scallop-edged scissors. Cut out the centres to make frames with narrow borders.

3 Glue the large frame to the lower part of the polka dot paper. Trace the heart templates at the back of the book. Cut out one large heart and one small heart from light pink vellum, and one medium heart and one small heart each from red vellum and dark pink paper. Glue the small hearts down the left-hand side and the medium hearts to the right above the large frame.

4 Glue the large pink heart to the middle of the page. Glue the small frames over the small hearts and glue the photographs in position in the frames.

VARIATION: **Other special occasions**

Right: This mosaic treatment is a good way to include plenty of individual shots of people who attend a farewell party. The scrapbook album page is a perfect record of those who attended as well as a good reminder of the occasion.

Far right: To mark the occasion of being voted lord mayor, this scrapbook album page is decorated with appropriately sombre colours.

Below: A handmade album cover for a special wedding anniversary is decorated with a ribbon of satin roses. The matt cream textured boards are appropriate for the subject.

Christmas celebrations

It's a treat to use the traditional festive colours of green and red for a Christmas layout, and deep red velvet-effect paper creates a fabulous rich background. Add plenty of gold and glitter for a thoroughly opulent look.

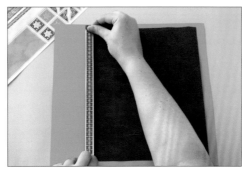

1 Cut a rectangle measuring 28 × 22.5cm/ 11 × 9in from the red velvet-effect paper and glue it to the green card, leaving a narrow border of green at the top, bottom and right-hand side.

2 Use a tartan border sticker to decorate the left-hand edge of the red velvet paper, sticking it centrally along the join.

materials and equipment

- red velvet-effect paper
- ruler
- pencil
- scissors
- spray adhesive
- 30cm/12in square sheet of green card (stock)
- tartan border sticker
- sheet of gold glitter card (stock)
- Christmas photograph
- fancy-edged scissors
- glue dots
- star punch
- oval cutter
- gold paper ribbon

VARIATION: Digital Christmas

Online scrapbooking stores offer a host of backgrounds and other ingredients for seasonally themed digital pages, so it's very easy to put together a page including pictures of your Christmas festivities. You could even add pictures of the children opening their presents and email it to friends and family on the big day itself.

3 Cut a piece of gold glitter card slightly larger all around than the photograph. Trim the edge using fancy-edged scissors. Glue the photograph to the gold card then glue in place on the background.

4 Using the tree template at the back of the book cut a Christmas tree out of green card. Punch some stars from gold card and glue in place. Glue the tree to the background. Cut three gold oval baubles and punch a hole near one end of each for threading a short length of paper ribbon through. Glue all the decorations in place.

Thanksgiving

A collection of vintage scraps and a row of patches cut from homespun fabrics embody the traditional values of American Thanksgiving celebrations, suggesting comfort and warmth. A brown paper background and manila photo corners add to the old-time feeling of this autumnal page.

materials and equipment

- spray adhesive
- 20 x 30cm/8 x 12in rectangle of blue craft paper
- 30cm/12in square sheet of brown card (stock)
- scissors
- narrow double-sided tape
- striped ribbon
- 4 shirt buttons
- red thread and needle
- 2 portrait format photographs
- 8 manila photo corners
- reproduction Thanksgiving scraps and photocopies
- glue stick
- skeleton leaves
- check cotton fabric scraps

1 Glue the blue craft paper to the centre of the background card. Cut two strips of double-sided tape and stick them over the two joins. Peel the protective layer from the tape and stick down two 32cm/13in lengths of ribbon, overlapping 1cm/½in at each end.

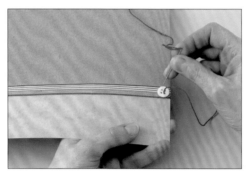

2 Turn the ends of ribbon to the wrong side and stick them down. Sew on a button at each end of the ribbons using red thread. Stitch through the card as well as the ribbon and fasten off securely on the back.

3 Arrange the two photographs on the blue section of the background, then attach them to the page with photo corners.

4 If you do not have enough original scraps, you can photocopy them, adjusting the sizes as necessary. Try reversing some copies to create a greater variety of images for the collage. Cut out the images accurately.

5 Arrange the scraps on the page and glue lightly in place with a glue stick. Don't stick down the edges at this stage.

6 Slip a few skeleton leaves in among the scraps. When you are happy with the arrangement, stick down both the leaves and the scraps securely.

7 Cut out several small fabric squares, following the grain of the fabric carefully to create an accurate shape. Gently pull away a few threads from each side to create fringed edges.

8 Arrange the fabric pieces evenly along the brown section at the lower edge of the page and stick down using a glue stick, leaving the fringed edges free.

Hannukah

The lighting of candles is an important part of the celebration of Hannukah, the Jewish festival of light. For impact, use one large photograph to fill one of the pages of this double-page spread. The title is arranged over both pages and uses a variety of letter styles. Metal embellishments with a Hannukah theme are available from scrapbooking suppliers.

materials and equipment

- 30cm/12in square sheet of pale blue card (stock)
- pencil
- scissors
- scrap paper
- patterned rubber stamp
- clear embossing stamp pad
- silver embossing powder
- heat tool
- 2 x 30cm/12in square sheets of navy blue card (stock)
- spray adhesive
- die-cut machine
- large label die
- 3 metal embellishments
- pale blue sheer ribbon
- assorted chipboard letters
- glue dots

1 Draw a capital "H" on pale blue card and cut it out. Rest it on a sheet of scrap paper and stamp it randomly using a patterned stamp and clear embossing fluid.

2 Place the pattern-stamped letter on a clean sheet of paper folded in the centre and sprinkle it liberally with silver embossing powder. (The paper will catch the excess powder and make it easier to pour back into the container.)

3 Using the heat tool, heat the embossing powder until it turns from powdery to shiny. Keep the tool moving to avoid scorching the card.

4 Glue the photograph in the centre of one of the navy blue sheets. Cut two 2.5cm/1in strips of pale blue card. Stick one down the left side of the page, centred in the margin. Trim the decorated initial and glue it at lower right, overlapping the photo.

5 Use a die-cut machine to cut out three labels from pale blue card. Alternatively, make a template and cut out three labels by hand.

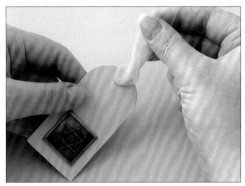

6 Attach the metal embellishments to the tags using glue dots. Cut three lengths of ribbon to loop through the top of each tag.

7 Arrange the remaining assorted letters along the bottom of the second page of the layout to finish the title. Make sure the heavy letters are firmly secured.

8 Stick the remaining pale blue strip acoss the top of the second page. Place the three decorated tags in a row below it and use glue dots to attach them firmly to the card.

Mum's birthday

If the children have made a special effort to surprise their mum on her birthday, that's definitely worth recording in style. The tiny envelopes on this layout can conceal a few mementoes or additional pictures of the day.

materials and equipment

- 30cm/12in square sheet of pale blue card (stock)
- pencil and metal ruler
- craft knife and cutting mat
- pink, white, lilac, light yellow and light green paper
- glue stick
- pair of compasses
- scissors
- flower punch
- tracing paper
- white, pink and lilac card (stock)
- small coin
- eyelet punch and eyelets
- photograph
- narrow organza ribbon

1 Draw a rectangle 15 × 10cm/6 × 4in on the blue card, 9.5cm/3¾in from the top and bottom edges, and 6cm/2½in in from the right edge. Cut out the rectangle using a craft knife and a metal ruler.

2 Cut a 20 × 15cm/8 × 6in rectangle of pale pink paper. Glue the paper to the back of the card, over the aperture.

3 Cut two 5cm/2in strips of white paper to fit across the page. Glue them in place, 2.5cm/1in in from the top and bottom edges, and trim any excess.

4 Draw and cut out eight 4cm/1¾in diameter circles of paper, two each in lilac, pink, light yellow and pale green. Glue the circles to the white strips. Punch eight flower shapes in the same colours and glue them in the centres of the circles.

5 Copy the envelope pattern at the back of the book on to thin white card and cut out to make a template. Draw around it once on pink and once on lilac card. Draw around a small coin twice on to pink card and twice on to lilac card. Cut them all out.

6 On the inside of the envelopes, score the fold lines and fold in the sides and flaps. Use an eyelet punch to make holes in the envelope flaps and the pink and lilac circles. Attach the circles to the flaps using eyelets.

7 Glue the photo in place inside the aperture, leaving equal amounts of pink border all round as a frame.

8 Glue the envelopes to the left side of the page, with the flaps to the front. Fill the envelopes, then fold in the sides and flaps and wrap a length of ribbon around the circles to keep the envelopes closed.

Father's Day

You could make this layout to honour your own or your children's father on Father's Day. The little pull-out book attached to the page means that the journaling can be kept for his eyes only: get the children to write in the book.

materials and equipment

- 3 x 30cm/12in square sheets of blue card (stock)
- 29cm/11½in square sheet of burgundy card (stock)
- tape runner
- 30 x 15cm/12 x 6in sheet of Argyll patterned paper
- photograph
- scissors
- silver embossing metal
- eyelet punch
- hammer
- screw brad
- metal ruler
- medium embossing tool
- pencil
- glue dots
- 30cm/12in burgundy ribbon
- 3 pale blue buttons

1 Glue the burgundy card on to a sheet of blue card, leaving an even margin all round. Attach the Argyll patterned paper across the top half of the page. Cut out a piece of blue card a little larger than the photograph and mat the picture with it. Mount the photo towards the top left corner of the album page so that there is room below it for further decoration.

2 Cut out an L-shaped piece of silver embossing metal to make a photo corner. Use an eyelet punch to make a small hole in the centre. Push the screw brad through and bend open the fasteners. Place in the top right corner of the layout.

3 Cut a 9.5cm/3½in square of embossing metal. Lay it on top of a spare piece of patterned paper and emboss it by laying a ruler along the lines of the design and scoring with the embossing tool.

4 To make the book, lightly mark the remaining sheet of blue card at 10cm/4in intervals along each edge. Fold up the first third using the marked edge as a guide. Crease the fold.

5 Fold the remaining third back the other way to make an accordion fold.

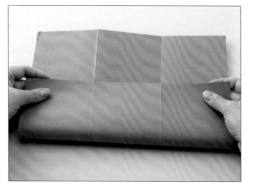

6 Unfold and turn the card through 90 degrees. Repeat the two folds in the other direction. Unfold again.

7 You should now have nine equal squares. Using scissors, cut out the top right square and the bottom left square.

8 Fold the top left corner square to cover the centre square and crease sharply.

9 Flip the card over and repeat with the opposite corner.

10 The sheet can now be folded naturally into a square book shape, opening from left to right.

11 Attach the embossed metal cover to the front of the book using glue dots.

12 Stick a length of ribbon across the back of the book. This will be used to tie the book shut. Attach the book to your page using glue dots.

13 To complete the layout, attach the three buttons using glue dots.

Weddings

The history of wedding photography is almost as long as that of photography itself, as couples began to visit the photographer's studio for a picture to commemorate their marriage as early as the 1840s. However, the limits of technology meant that the camera did not leave the studio to cover the whole affair until the boom in weddings almost a century later.

It was not until the 1970s that the formal posed photographic style gave way to a more relaxed approach. Since then, weddings have been portrayed in a much more journalistic style, and the traditional album of posed shots is also giving way to much freer treatments, for which the skills of scrapbooking are extremely well suited. Many small reminders of the big day, such as menus, confetti and flowers from the bouquet, can now take their place in an album that captures the whole atmosphere of the wedding in a unique way.

A traditional wedding

This lovely reminder of a special day, featuring the wedding photograph and invitation, and decorated with cut-out doves and hearts, is simple yet effective in black, white and gold. This page can be the first in a wedding album, to be followed by other pictures of the happy day.

materials and equipment

- spiral-bound album
- craft knife
- metal ruler
- cutting mat
- heavy white paper
- fancy-edged scissors
- translucent glassine paper
- glue stick
- wedding photograph
- transparent photo corners
- scissors
- pencil
- gold paper
- gold card (stock)
- translucent envelope
- wedding mementoes: invitation, pressed flowers, ribbon, confetti

1 Before starting work on the layout itself, make a protective page for the treasured photograph by cutting the preceding page out of the album to within about 2.5cm/1in of the spiral binding. Use a craft knife and a metal ruler, and work on a cutting mat.

2 Cut another strip of paper slightly wider than the first strip from a sheet of heavy white paper. Trim one long edge with fancy-edged scissors. Cut a sheet of glassine paper or other translucent paper the same size as the album pages to replace the page you have removed.

3 Glue the glassine paper to the tab in the album, then cover this with the single strip of paper with the decorative edge visible. The translucent protective sheet should now be sandwiched between the two tabs. Allow to dry.

4 Assemble the photograph display. Using fancy-edged scissors, cut around the edges of a piece of heavy white paper slightly larger than the photograph. Mount the photo on this using transparent photo corners.

VARIATION: Family weddings

Many family photograph collections include formal pictures of relatives' weddings, copies of which were usually ordered from the professional photographer and sent out to guests or to those unable to attend the wedding. Often these pictures are to be found, years later, tucked into a drawer or in a box of miscellaneous prints. Yet they are an important part of your family history, as well as being fascinating glimpses of the past, and deserve to be properly presented in your albums.

If old photographs include wedding guests unknown to you, try to find out who they are from older family members and gather all the information you can about the day. The page you design can include journaling to preserve all these memories. In the case of more recent events that you attended yourself, you can include souvenirs such as the invitation and order of service.

It's nice to design the page in a way that is appropriate to the period and the style of the wedding: you can usually get plenty of ideas from the clothes worn by the guests and the settings of the photographs. Many of these will be in black and white so will look best against subtly coloured backgrounds.

5 Copy the dove and heart templates at the back of the book and cut them out. Draw round them on the wrong side of gold paper and heavy white paper. Reverse the dove motif so that they face in different directions. Cut them out.

6 To assemble the album page, stick down a piece of gold card slightly larger than the mounted photo. Add a translucent envelope containing a memento of the occasion such as an invitation, together with any other small saved pressed flowers, ribbon, confetti or similar. Place some of the motifs you have cut out inside the envelope too. Glue down the mounted photograph. Stick the dove and heart cut-outs on to the page in a pleasing arrangement.

An Indian wedding

Traditional Indian weddings are celebrated on a huge scale, with a great deal of ritual, and hundreds of guests are often invited and lavishly entertained. The ceremony is full of vibrant colour and sparkle, with splendid clothes, flowers and food, and provides plenty of visual inspiration for a gorgeous album page ornamented in red and gold.

1 Cut a rectangle of starry tissue paper measuring 30 x 10cm/12 x 4in and use spray adhesive to stick it to the sheet of gold card 7.5cm/3in from the top edge.

2 Cut a 10cm/4in square of red embroidered paper. Glue it to the tissue paper panel on the left side of the page, matching the edges.

3 Cut a length of gold braid and another of sequins to fit along the top and bottom of the panel and glue them in place. Glue the photograph in the centre of the panel.

materials and equipment

- gold tissue with star pattern
- metal ruler and pencil
- craft knife and cutting mat
- 30cm/12in square sheet of thin gold card (stock)
- spray adhesive
- red embroidered paper
- fringed gold braid
- sequin strip
- PVA (white) glue
- 10cm/4in square photograph
- thin white card (stock)
- eyelet punch
- gold, red and green flower sequins
- star-shaped eyelets
- red and green shiny paper
- heart paper punch
- thin paper in gold and red
- small photos and mementoes
- gold marker pen
- thin gold ribbon

4 To make the folders, cut three rectangles of thin white card each 16 x 8cm/6 x 3in. Lightly score a line down the rectangles, 4cm/1½in from each side. Fold the scored lines to make flaps.

5 Punch a hole in the centre of each flap using an eyelet punch. Punch matching holes in two gold flower sequins. Attach the sequins to the flaps with star-shaped eyelets. Repeat for the other two folders.

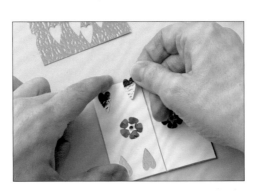

6 Punch eight hearts for each folder from red or green shiny paper. Stick the hearts to the flaps of the folders, four on each door.

7 Cut two squares of red embroidered paper and one of thin gold paper to fit inside the folders and glue them in place. Draw a heart template to fit inside the squares and use it to cut out two gold and one red paper heart. Glue them into the folders and stick mementoes or photos of the bride and groom to the gold hearts.

8 Inscribe the names of the bride and groom in gold on the red heart. Glue the folders in position on the page, beneath the border, with the red heart in the centre. Cut three lengths of gold ribbon and tie the ribbon through the holes in the sequins to keep the flaps closed.

A contemporary wedding

Using computer-printed kisses and light, bright colours, this layout reflects a modern take on a timeless ceremony, inspired by the unconventional wedding group photograph that forms its centrepiece. You could add some text to some of the panels instead of the printed kisses if you prefer.

materials and equipment

- 30cm/12in square sheet of white card (stock)
- computer and printer
- tracing paper
- metal ruler
- pencil
- craft knife
- cutting mat
- spray adhesive
- lilac, turquoise, blue, green and cream paper
- scissors
- glue stick
- heart punch

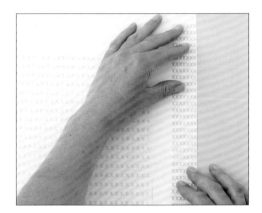

1 Print kisses on to two sheets of tracing paper. Trim the paper to size. Glue to the white card with spray adhesive to make decorative areas.

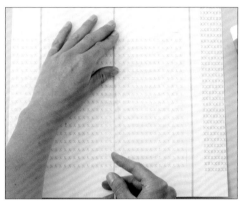

2 Cut three 30cm x 3mm/12 x ⅛in strips of lilac paper. Glue one strip down the middle of the card. Glue the remaining strips at each side of the card, 5cm/2in in from the edges.

3 Cut a selection of rectangles and ovals on to turquoise, lilac, blue and green paper. Cut them all out.

4 Assemble the layered shapes, gluing one colour on top of another.

5 Print the bride and groom's names and large kisses on to tracing paper. Trim them to size and glue them to the rectangles and ovals.

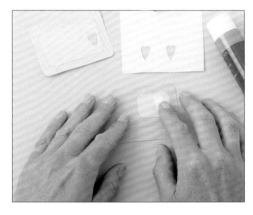

6 Punch hearts from cream, lilac and blue paper. Glue them to the rectangles.

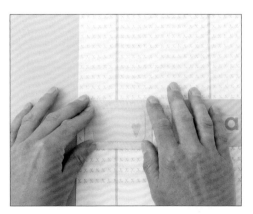

7 Arrange the rectangles down the lilac "strings", then glue them in place.

8 Trim the photo to size, rounding the corners. Glue it in place.

Heritage wedding

A heritage treatment for an old wedding photograph requires the use of colours and embellishments that are appropriate to the period of the picture. For this layout, fabrics and flowers in muted tones create a delicate background, and the look is subtle and stylish. Pieced calico was used here, but plain undyed fabric would be equally effective.

materials and equipment

- pieced natural calico fabric
- dressmaker's scissors
- 3 x 30cm/12in square sheets of kraft card (stock)
- spray adhesive
- large wedding photograph
- 30cm/12in square sheet of cream card (stock)
- craft knife and metal ruler
- cutting mat
- wide sheer cream ribbon
- jewelled stick pin
- pen and plain paper
- cork mat
- paper piercer or bodkin
- small pearl beads
- moulded paper flowers
- dimensional glaze
- stranded embroidery thread (floss) in cream
- needle
- sticky tabs

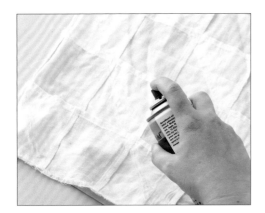

1 Cut two 32cm/12¾in squares of calico to create the backgrounds for the pages. Cover one sheet of kraft card completely with the fabric, attaching it with spray adhesive and turning the raw edges to the back of the sheet. Cut the second fabric square approximately in half, cutting in a gentle serpentine shape, then glue it to a second sheet of kraft card, leaving the right-hand side of the card bare.

2 Double-mat the wedding photograph on a sheet of kraft card and a larger sheet of cream card. Tie a loop of sheer cream ribbon to fit over the corner of the photograph and glue it at the back. Tie the ends into a bow at the front. Stick a jewelled stick pin through the knot of the ribbon bow. Attach the photograph to the centre of the left-hand page.

3 To create the title, write the word "Wedding" or the names of the bride and groom in a flowing script on a piece of plain paper. Place the uncovered area of the right-hand page on a cork mat with the inscribed paper on top and prick evenly through the paper and the card using a paper piercer or bodkin, following the written line.

4 Attach a pearl bead to the centre of each paper flower using dimensional glaze. Use a minimal amount of glaze, and leave it to dry thoroughly before attaching the flowers to the layout.

5 Glue individual flowers down the pages following the lines of the pieced fabric, and in a line following the curved side of the fabric to cover the raw edge. Attach three more flowers to the card at the foot of the right-hand page. Stitch the title with three strands of embroidery thread, using back stitch and following the pre-pricked holes.

6 On the back of the page, secure the ends of the thread with sticky tabs rather than tying knots, as these might create indentations visible from the front.

Our wedding day

A brightly coloured wedding dress and a fun photograph were the inspiration for this jolly layout, a radical departure from traditional wedding album pages. The red bodice of the dress was decorated with bold flowers and these motifs have been repeated in the page embellishments.

materials and equipment

- 2 x 30cm/12in square sheets white card (stock)
- craft knife and metal ruler
- cutting mat
- 2 x 30cm/12in square sheets red card (stock)
- spray adhesive
- large wedding photograph
- die-cut machine
- selection of flower dies
- large and extra large circle punches
- dark pink card (stock)
- medium pink card (stock)
- foam pads
- large and extra large daisy punches
- glue pen
- rub-on letters in pink
- embossing tool

1 To make the background, trim one sheet of white card and glue it to a red sheet to leave a narrow border of red all round. Mat the photograph on red card and attach to the background towards the top right. Die-cut a selection of flower shapes and circles in red, pink and white card. Mix and match the flowers, centres and circles and glue them together.

2 Attach foam pads to the backs of some of the completed embellishments to raise them on the page. Arrange all the flowers along the left side of the photograph so that they overlap. Stick in position.

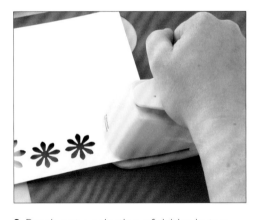

3 Punch out a selection of daisies in two sizes and in different colours.

4 Using a glue pen, stick the small daisies to the centres of the large daisies, mixing the colours. Leave to dry.

5 Place the daisies around and between the other flower embellishments and glue in position on the page.

◄ 6 Apply the rub-on letters using an embossing tool, and position the title in the lower right area of the page below the photograph. Rub on the last letter first: this will ensure that you get the spacing correct and the word will not run off the page.

BESSIE LOVE.

Family history

A heritage album is a delightful way to document your family's unique history and to preserve old photographs and mementoes for future generations. Most families have boxes of photographs just waiting to be unearthed and sorted out, and this in itself can be a fascinating journey back in time, particularly if you can ask your older relatives to help you identify the faces of long-lost family members and friends.

When you come to make selections of photographs for your pages, portraits and special occasions such as weddings and family parties will be central features, but try to include other shots that set them in context, such as pictures showing your forebears' houses or places of work, cars, gardens and home towns.

Family tree

This is a great way to record your family tree. Instead of drawing a diagram of names and dates, this family tree is decorated with pictures of each family member, glued on paper leaves with their details added alongside.

materials and equipment

- selection of family photographs or reprints
- scissors
- paper or card for template
- pencil
- paper in two shades of green
- glue stick
- sheet of marble-effect paper
- small labels
- pen
- green mount board (optional)

1 Re-photograph the pictures on sepia-effect or black and white film, or scan them and convert to monotone or duotone, ensuring that all the faces are a similar size. Cut out each portrait carefully.

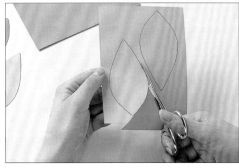

2 Make a leaf template and draw around it on the wrong side of a piece of green paper. Cut around the outline. Repeat to make a leaf background for each picture, using paper in two shades of green.

3 Glue a photograph on to each leaf and allow to dry. Trim away the excess photograph to fit the leaf shape.

4 Arrange the pictures on the marble paper background, with the youngest generation at the bottom. Glue in place. Next to each photograph stick a label on which to add names and dates. If desired, mount the family tree on green mount board to finish.

FAMILY CARS

Since the early days of the twentieth century, the car has been a prized family possession. Looking back through snapshots from holidays and outings over the years, you will find they crop up in pictures of your grandmother, father or aunt just as frequently as in those of younger relatives. Sort out all the photographs featuring cars, whether they are parked at picnics, driving along distant roads or being towed away on a breakdown truck, to make a record of your family motoring.

materials and equipment

- old road maps
- photocopier
- sheet of card (stock)
- glue stick
- driving handbooks
- scissors
- selection of photographs

1 Photocopy the maps on the lightest setting. Stick them to the card to make the background, overlapping them so that all the card is concealed. Copy images of road signs from old driving handbooks or maps and cut them out.

2 Arrange the pictures on the page, leaving space at the top and centre right. Glue lines of road sign cut-outs in these spaces, on bands of coloured paper if necessary so that they show up clearly. Stick down all the photographs using a glue stick.

Victorian scrap album page

Having a formal studio photograph taken was an important event for past generations, when cameras were prohibitively expensive and required the special skills of a professional photographer to operate them. The resulting portraits – like this charming oval picture – were framed and treasured. You can update an old family photograph in this way, or print out a contemporary picture in sepia to create a period-style picture.

materials and equipment

- original or reproduction sheet of coloured scraps
- photocopier
- scissors
- oval photograph
- 30cm/12in square sheet of coloured card (stock)
- paper glue
- paper doily
- coloured paper

1 Photocopy the sheet of scraps, enlarging them if you wish. Make a second copy, this time with the image reversed (use the "iron-on" paper setting on your printer or ask your local copy shop to do this for you). Cut out each image carefully around the outline with small scissors, taking care to cut away all the white background.

2 Cut out the photograph if necessary and glue it centrally to the background. Arrange the scraps around it, placing the mirror images on opposite sides. Overlap them to form a solid border, and glue them in place when you are pleased with the results. By adding a few that break out of the frame you will give movement to the design.

3 Choose a motif from the paper doily for the corner decoration. It should be a part of the design that is repeated so that you can use it four times, and should be about 5cm/2in high. Cut out the four motifs roughly and glue a piece of coloured paper to the wrong side of each. Cut out the paper following the outline of the motif.

VARIATION: Découpage boxes

If you have a collection of small trifles and keepsakes that have been handed down to you, give them safekeeping in a pretty box decorated with Victorian-style découpage. Plain cardboard boxes ideal for this purpose are available from craft suppliers in many shapes and sizes. Cut out small reproduction scraps of flowers, cherubs, butterflies and other pretty subjects, taking care to remove any white background, which would distract from the overall colourful effect, and glue them, overlapping, all over the base and lid. Apply several coats of glossy varnish to give a rich antique look.

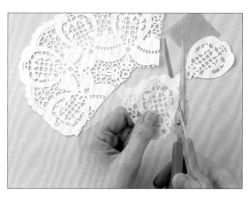

4 Stick one motif down near each corner of the background, pointing the designs towards the centre. Cut out eight more small matching shapes from the paper doily and glue a pair to each side of each corner shape to finish the decoration.

Remember when...

This heritage layout has a homespun look to it that suits the rustic scene in the old photograph. It has been achieved by using neutral colours, fabric, hand-stitching and twill tape printed with a nostalgic message. Photographs showing relatives at work are usually rarer than those depicting family and friends, and a good subject to record for posterity.

1 Mat the photograph on cream card. Place it on a cork mat and pierce holes, evenly spaced, all round the mat. Work a running stitch through the holes to make a border.

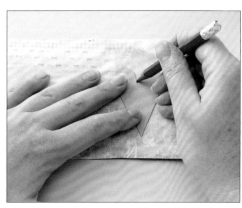

2 Cut a heart shape from scrap card to make a template. Iron fusible bonding web to the wrong side of the fabric. Draw round the template on the backing sheet and cut out five fabric hearts.

materials and equipment

- old photograph
- 30cm/12in square sheet of cream card (stock)
- craft knife
- metal ruler
- cutting mat
- spray adhesive
- cork mat
- paper piercer or bodkin
- stranded embroidery thread (floss) in cream
- needle
- scissors
- fusible bonding web
- patterned cotton fabric
- iron
- 30cm/12in square sheet of dark kraft card (stock)
- tape runner
- printed twill tape
- small brown buttons in two sizes
- glue dots

3 Arrange the hearts in a row across the bottom of the layout and use a tape runner to stick them in place.

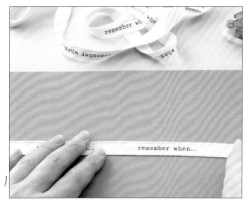

4 Cut two lengths of printed twill tape and stick them to the layout, one 10cm/4in from the top and the other below the row of hearts. Attach the photograph to the layout, gluing it over the upper length of tape.

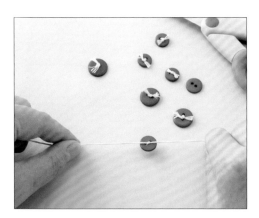

5 Tie stranded embroidery thread through the holes in the buttons. Trim to leave short ends and fluff out the strands.

6 Attach the buttons to the tape between the printed words, using glue dots, and add more buttons beside the photograph.

7 Pierce two holes on each side of and through each heart and stitch with three strands of embroidery thread.

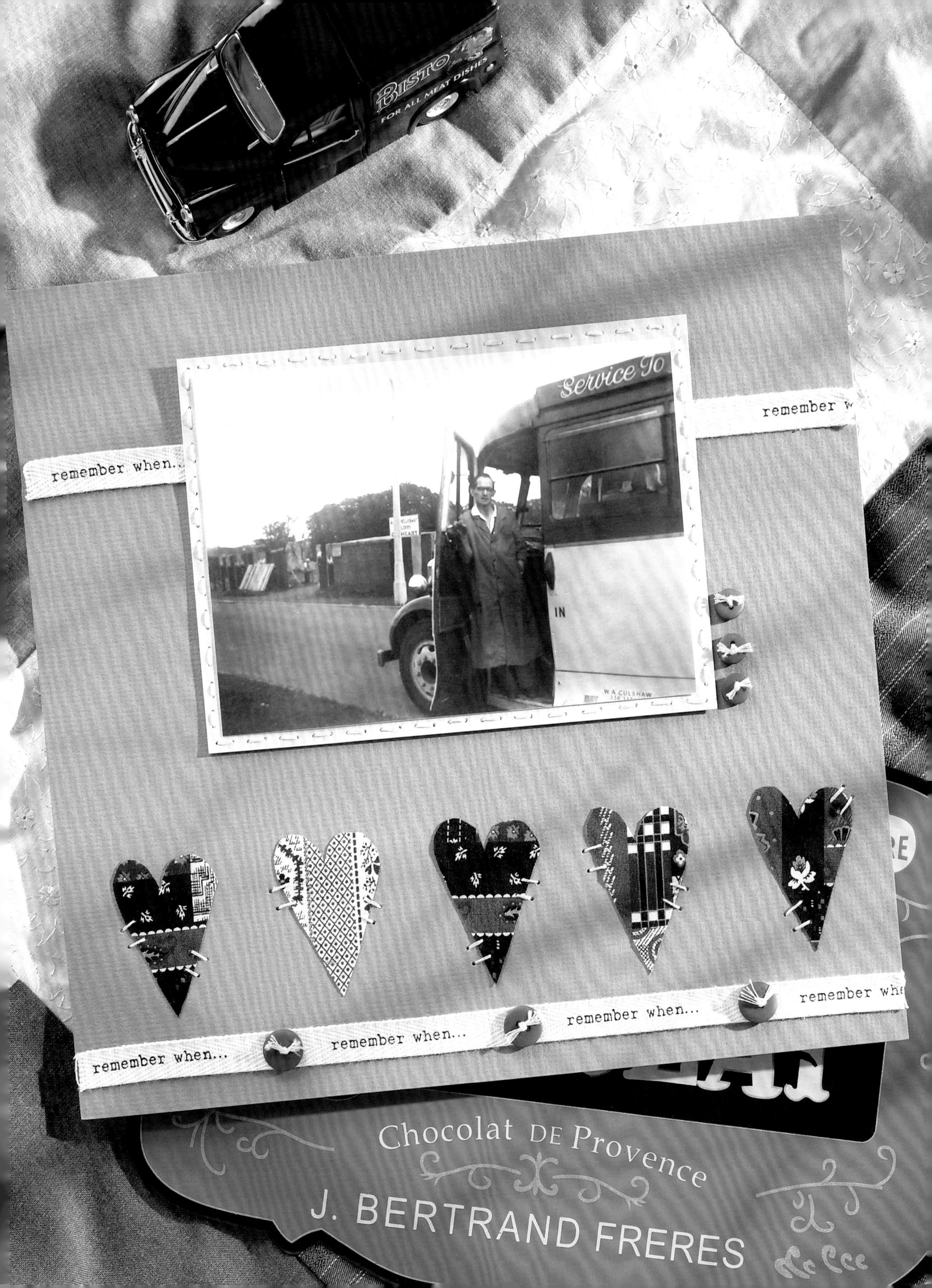
BISTO
FOR ALL MEAT DISHES
Service To
remember when...
remember wh
IN
W.A.CULSHAW
remember when...
remember when...
remember when...
remember whe
Chocolat DE Provence
J. BERTRAND FRERES

Mother and child

This evocative sepia print of a serene mother and her robust baby boy, taken in 1909, is faded and fragile, and has to be stored carefully away from the light. To preserve the memory, it was copied and enlarged at a slightly darker setting, then cropped to remove the damaged area. The "shabby chic" style used for this layout is perfect for very old family photographs.

materials and equipment

- 35cm/14in length of fine lace, 10cm/4in wide
- scissors
- iron
- spray adhesive
- 30cm/12in square sheet of kraft card (stock)
- piece of floral-patterned fabric
- photocopier
- white A4 paper
- photograph
- glue stick
- tracing paper and pencil
- heavy pink paper
- letters and other ephemera
- 2 Victorian scraps or other pictures
- tiny paper flowers

1 Press the lace to remove any creases and trim the raw edge. Spray the wrong side with spray adhesive, and attach to the lower part of the background card with the scalloped edge facing downwards. Fold the ends of the lace to the back of the card and stick down.

2 Photocopy the fabric on to A4 paper, setting the printer to a lighter than normal setting to give a faded appearance to the design. Glue to the upper part of the background so that the lower edge lies along the top of the lace.

3 Enlarge the photograph so that it is about 17.5cm/7in high, trimming off any areas that were damaged in the original and darkening the print if necessary. Using spray adhesive, stick it down on the right-hand side of the floral paper.

4 Trace the envelope template at the back of the book on to tracing paper and transfer it to heavy pink paper. Cut out, then fold all four flaps to the centre along the broken lines. Glue the bottom flap to the side flaps.

5 Stick the front of the envelope to the layout at the lower left. Fill the envelope with letters, postcards and other ephemera, displaying them so that the stamps and addresses face outwards.

6 Glue the two scraps in place, one on each side of the page.

7 Finish off the layout by gluing a scattering of tiny paper flowers across the page.

VARIATION: Family group

For this more recent photograph of a mother and her children, a more abstract setting has been chosen, using layers of torn paper in a subtle blend of buff and brick red inspired by the marbled paper used as the background. A black border around the picture adds definition to the rather soft grey tones of the photograph, and the assortment of letters in the title includes some black and white to match the central subject.

Edwardian childhood

The formal clothing of Edwardian childhood – bonnets, buttoned boots, frilly petticoats and fitted jackets – and the strict routine of the classroom were balanced by hours spent playing in the nursery with dolls, dolls' houses, toy cars and train sets. Record this lost era with a family photograph, pages from copy books and engravings from a contemporary shopping catalogue.

materials and equipment

- hand-marbled paper
- craft knife and metal ruler
- cutting mat
- 30cm/12in square sheet of white card (stock)
- spray adhesive
- photograph
- scanner and printer
- white paper
- scissors
- gummed black paper photo corners
- photocopier
- old copy book
- glue stick
- old engravings of toys

1 Cut a square of marbled paper to fit the background sheet, and stick in place with spray adhesive.

2 Enlarge the photograph so that it measures about 16cm/6½in high. Alter the brightness and colour balances if necessary to enhance the image if it is faded. Slip four old-fashioned paper photo corners on to the picture and place it in position on the left side of the layout.

3 Photocopy and cut out four pages from an old handwriting copy book. Cut two narrow strips from one of the pages.

4 Arrange the other three pages on the right side of the page so that they overlap each other and the edge of the layout.

5 Place one of the copy book strips at the top and one at the bottom of the left side and glue in place.

6 Cut out engraved images of dolls, train sets, rocking horses and other toys, cutting as close as possible to the outer edges.

7 Arrange all the toys on the layout over the background and the copy book pages.

8 Double check the position of all the various elements and when you are pleased with the design, glue everything securely in place.

University revue

Your pictures may not always be the perfect shape for square album pages. This production photograph from a student musical sums up all the glamour and excitement of amateur dramatics, but the upright, portrait format is not ideal. With a little photocopying and clever cutting, however, a single dancer can be turned into a chorus line that fills the stage.

materials and equipment

- theatrical photograph
- photocopier
- white paper
- scissors
- glue stick
- curtain from toy theatre kit
- heavy red paper
- wavy-edged scissors
- old sheet music
- 30cm/12in square sheet of gold card (stock)
- tracing paper
- pencil
- scraps of thin black and gold card (stock)

1 Photocopy the image five times, enlarging it if necessary. Cut around the figure to be reproduced on four of the copies. Glue the pictures together so that the figures overlap realistically.

2 Cut out the printed curtain from a toy theatre kit, or cut out a paper curtain shape, and glue it to the top of the picture. Mat the picture on a square of red paper trimmed with wavy-edged scissors.

3 Cut four strips from a page of old sheet music and mount them on the back of the red paper to form a square frame. Glue to the centre of a sheet of gold card.

4 Trace the spotlight template at the back of the book and use it to cut out two spotlight silhouettes from black card and two oval discs from gold card. Glue the discs to the lights and fix in position at the top corners of the music.

VARIATION: Period detail

A page photocopied from an illustrated trade catalogue of the appropriate period makes a fascinating and evocative background for a heritage layout.

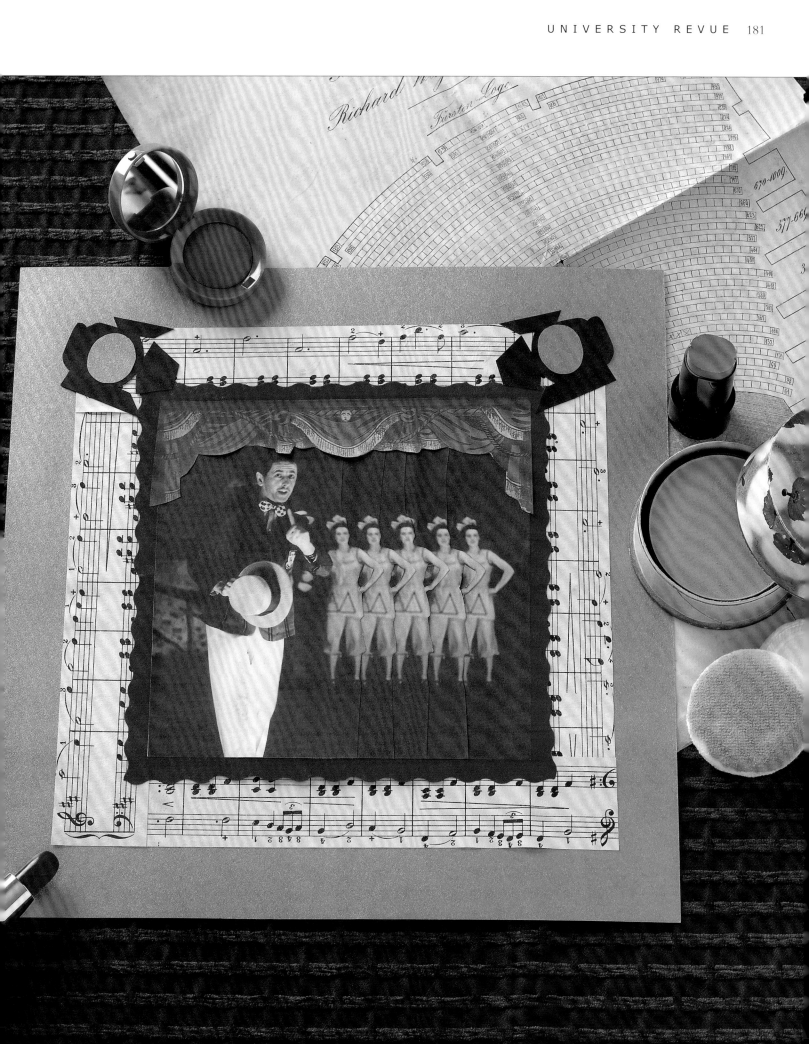

Family and friends

Happy times spent with your nearest and dearest are perfect subjects for your album pages, and you can include lots of informal snapshots of adults and children having fun and just being themselves – a world away from the formal posed photographs taken at special events such as weddings. For these pages you can go out armed with a camera with possible layouts already in mind, ready to look out for good subjects for backgrounds and embellishments as well as the focal points of the pages.

If you discuss your ideas with your friends and relatives you might also be able to get them to co-operate by posing together, larking about for action shots or even dressing up. If you have a digital camera you can easily take lots of pictures to give you plenty of choice at your next scrapbooking session. And if they know they've been involved, your friends will be eager to see themselves immortalized on the resulting pages.

Picnic in the park

This fun collage combines snapshots of an al fresco *picnic with cut-outs of cutlery, wine bottles, plates and a picnic basket to tell the story of a good outing. This is a really enjoyable and simple way to record a memorable day; you could make similar pages about a trip to the zoo or a child's birthday party by creating collages in the same style. It's worth building up a stock of cuttings by saving promising pages from magazines with good colour photography. Alternatively, when you're snapping away during a picnic, take some pictures of small details such as the basket, rug, bottles and food, as well as general shots of your surroundings for the background.*

materials and equipment

- magazine pages with pictures of picnic items
- scissors
- sheet of green paper
- glue stick
- snapshots of a family picnic
- transparent photo corners

1 Assemble the motifs for the design. Carefully and accurately cut out pictures of a picnic basket, picnic rug, plates, cutlery, glasses and food, using sharp scissors. Ensure there is no background showing once you have completed the cutting out.

2 Glue a picture of a travel rug down in one corner of the green background paper. Arrange photographs of the picnic on the paper, and when you are happy with the design, attach the pictures to the page with transparent photo corners.

3 Arrange the other cut-outs decoratively around the photographs to fill in the spaces. Some cut-outs can be placed on the rug, and others displayed in groups scattered around the picnic photographs. Glue them all in place.

VARIATIONS: Family outings

Below: Memories of childhood trips to the seaside invariably invoke pangs of nostalgia for traditional pleasures such as building sandcastles, eating ice creams and paddling in the sea, while the grown-ups looked on from their deck chairs. This digital album page captures the retro feel of those old memories by reproducing the photographs in a small square format with white borders like early colour prints. Behind them, an atmospheric photograph of a sandy beach is reproduced with a reduced opacity so that it fades into the background. A few marine embellishments complete the picture.

Above and Below: When you are portraying outings with children, include pictures of the animals or plants you saw as well as the children themselves, as reminders for them when they look at your album in future years.

Trip to the farm

In this small accordion album, photographs of a visit to a farm are mounted on tags slotted into pockets, and no child will be able to resist pulling them out to find his or her picture on each one. Close-up shots of crops and animals have been used to cover the pockets, conveying the flavour of the trip in near-abstract images that are all about texture and colour. A naive illustration created using rubber stamps provides the finishing touch.

materials and equipment

- 2 sheets of A4 card (stock) in lime green
- tracing paper
- pencil
- metal ruler
- craft knife
- cutting mat
- self-cling unmounted stamps
- clear acrylic block
- coloured ink pads
- gift wrap or magazine pages
- glue stick
- daisy punch
- white paper
- eyelet punch and eyelets
- thin card (stock) in pale blue, turquoise and lilac
- photographs
- narrow ribbon
- gift wrap

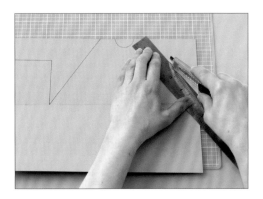

1 Fold one green card in half lengthwise. Press the fold firmly to make a sharp crease. Trace the album template at the back of the book and transfer the tracing to the green card, matching the central line to the crease. Cut out the album.

2 Fold the card where marked to create the album. Press all the folds firmly to make sharp creases.

3 Press the self-cling stamps one by one on to the acrylic block and stamp the flower and butterfly design on the large pocket.

4 Cut sections from gift wrap or pictures cut from magazines to fit the remaining pockets and glue in place.

5 Punch a small daisy from white paper.

6 Use an eyelet punch to make holes in the corners of the pockets, and in the daisy. Insert eyelets through the holes to fix the album together.

7 Trace the tag templates at the back of the book. Transfer the shapes to thin, coloured card and cut them out.

8 Punch four daisies from white paper. Glue one to the top of each tag.

9 Punch a hole through each daisy with an eyelet punch. Trim the photos to size and glue them to the tags.

10 Cut lengths of ribbon and tie one through the hole in the top of each tag.

11 Cut two covers slightly larger than the album from the remaining sheet of card and cover them with gift wrap. Glue the covers to the front and back of the album. Trim and glue photos to the front and back covers. Cut a length of ribbon and tie it around the album to keep it closed.

A day in the garden

Summer days are often spent in the garden, having lunch or a drink and chatting with family and friends. Keep a record of this part of life by making a collage using photos of your loved ones relaxing outside, decorated with stamped garden designs and pressed flowers and leaves.

materials and equipment

- selection of rubber stamps with a garden theme: plant pots, flowers, garden tools
- selection of papers in shades of green, brown and off-white
- ink pads in black and dark green
- paper towels
- fancy-edged scissors
- scissors
- photographs
- sheet of brown paper
- glue stick
- gummed brown paper photo corners
- selection of pressed flowers and leaves

1 Stamp several versions of garden-themed designs on a selection of coloured and textured paper, using black and dark green ink. Clean the stamps between different colours with paper towels. Allow to dry.

2 Cut out some of the stamped motifs with fancy-edged scissors and others with ordinary scissors. Tear around some of the motifs to create rough edges.

For a digital scrapbook page, create the feel of a summer garden with a photographic montage in fresh greens and blues. You can find themed collections on scrapbooking websites offering suitable colourful borders and embellishments such as these jolly sunglasses, or make up your own borders and collage elements using the image-editing software on your computer. In the example on the right, all the images were cropped from one photograph, then enlarged and superimposed for a montage effect. The simpler treatment below could be achieved equally easily in digital or traditional form.

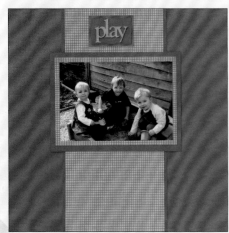

VARIATION: Summer in the garden

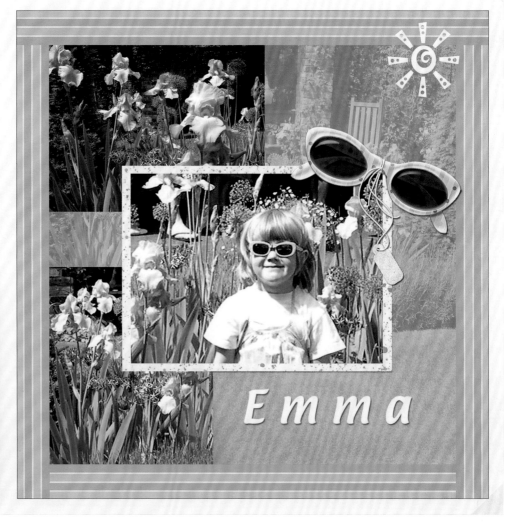

3 Arrange the photos on the foundation page. When you are happy with the arrangement, stick the pictures down with the photo corners.

4 Assemble the collage by adding the different stamped motifs, pressed flowers and leaves. Glue each item in position.

Gone fishing

Capture the magic of a long afternoon spent by the water's edge with this fun layout featuring a fond grandfather with his young grandson. Even if they didn't manage to hook anything with their makeshift rod, you can crop the photograph and add a catch consisting of a few embossed silver fish.

1 Cut a square of patterned paper to fit the background card and attach it with spray adhesive. Cut a 7.5cm/3in strip of dark blue paper to fit along the bottom of the page. Cut along the top edge with wavy-edged scissors and stick it in place.

2 Use the wavy-edged scissors to cut out a few "waves" from the pale blue paper and glue them at intervals across the "water".

materials and equipment

- patterned paper
- 30cm/12in square sheet of card (stock)
- spray adhesive
- craft knife
- metal ruler
- cutting mat
- thin paper in dark and pale blue
- wavy-edged scissors
- 2 photographs
- glue stick and sticky tape
- tracing paper
- fine waterproof pen
- silver embossing foil
- thick card or cork mat
- embossing tool or empty ballpoint pen
- old scissors
- large needle
- stranded embroidery thread (floss) in cream or fine string

3 Decide on the best position for the two photographs and stick them to the patterned background using a glue stick.

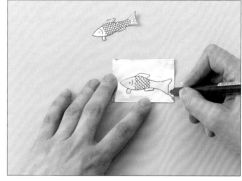

4 Trace the fish template at the back of the book and cut out around the outline. Cut a small rectangle of embossing foil and, using a fine waterproof pen, draw around the template, then fill in the detail.

5 Lay the foil on a piece of thick card or a cork mat and trace over the lines with a stylus or old ballpoint pen, pressing firmly.

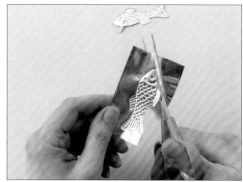

6 Use an old pair of scissors to cut out the fish. Make another three fish in the same way, reversing some of them so that they appear to swim in opposite directions.

7 Stick the fish to the dark blue paper with a glue stick, spacing them evenly between the waves.

8 Thread a large needle with thread or fine string. Bring the needle out at the tip of the fishing rod and take it back in close to the fish, allowing the thread to loop gently. Tape the ends to the wrong side.

Birthday party

Children's birthday parties are big events to organize so it's nice to have a record of the day, as well as of your children's favourite friends, so that you can see how the the celebrations and children change as the years pass.

materials and equipment

- selection of toning papers
- 6 photographs
- 30cm/12in square sheet of card (stock)
- cutting mat
- craft knife and metal ruler
- spray adhesive
- corner cutter
- purple metallic ink pad
- 5 tags
- glue dots
- stamp rubber stamp design
- flower and heart cutters
- brads
- sequins
- small floral stickers
- number template
- scissors

1 Choose a selection of toning papers in colours that match your photographs and the background card. Working on a cutting mat and using a craft knife and metal ruler, cut one 12.5cm/5in square and mat it to the top left-hand corner of the background.

2 Cut frames for your main photographs, 1cm/½in larger all around than the photographs. Use a corner cutter to trim the corners. Trim the photographs in the same way.

3 Tint the edge of the main photograph frame using a purple metallic ink pad. Allow to dry. Mat the photographs to the frames, then mat the frames in position on the background.

4 Choose different papers to cover each of the five gift tags. Working in a ventilated area and with scrap paper on the work surface, use spray adhesive to coat the tags and mat each to coloured paper. Allow to dry, then carefully cut each out.

5 Cut and trim three photographs and their corners to fit the tags. Cut slightly larger frames for each. Stick each of the three photographs to a frame, and a frame to a tag using glue dots or spray adhesive.

6 For a tag without a photograph, decorate a plain frame with a stamped design. Add stickers to decorate the other tag without a photograph.

7 Cut four flower motifs and one heart motif as additional decoration for the tags. Make a hole in the centre of each flower and in the top of four tags.

8 For the tags without photographs, thread a sequin on a brad, then a flower, a frame and a tag. Open out the wings of the brad. Stick the tag to the background.

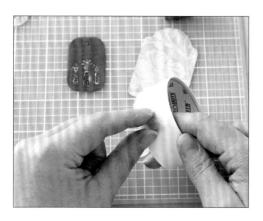

9 For the centre tag, stick a heart to the top of the frame. Decorate the remaining tags as you like.

10 Add small floral stickers to the background and the frames, as desired.

11 Cut out the child's age from coloured paper using a template. Decorate the edges with the ink pad as before. Stick in place.

Magic carpet

With a little imagination you can transform an ordinary afternoon in the garden into a fairytale fantasy. All you need is a photograph of your family or best friends sitting out in the sunshine and a picture of the hearthrug. When taking the photographs, get everyone to sit close together in a solid group, and photograph the rug from a low angle. Cut them out, mount them together on an idyllic blue sky and you have a magic carpet to take you all on a wonderful adventure.

materials and equipment

- group photograph
- computer and printer
- scissors
- photograph of rug
- hard and soft pencils
- tracing paper
- A4 sheet of thin silver card (stock)
- craft knife
- cutting mat
- scraps of coloured paper
- 60cm/24in metallic braid
- glue stick
- 30cm/12in square of sky-printed background paper
- tiny silver star stickers
- scrap of silver paper
- 4 small silver fabric motifs

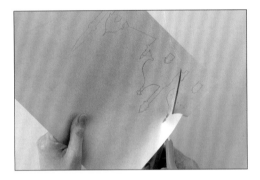

1 Enlarge the group photograph so that it measures approximately 15cm/6in from side to side and cut it out, following the outline of the figures as closely as you can.

2 Enlarge the picture of the carpet to about 25cm/10in wide and cut out carefully, eliminating the original background.

3 Trace the template from the back of the book, enlarging it to 30cm/12in wide. Transfer the outline to silver card. Cut along the skyline with scissors and cut out the windows with a craft knife on a cutting mat.

4 Glue a small piece of coloured paper behind each window opening.

5 Cut two lengths of metallic braid and glue them along the top and bottom edges of the sky-printed background sheet.

6 Stick the silhouette to the background, just above the braid. Glue the family picture on to the carpet, then move it around the card until you are happy with its position. Stick it in place using a glue stick.

7 Scatter the silver star stickers across the sky. Cut out a small crescent moon from silver paper and stick it low down in the sky near the buildings.

8 Stick a silver motif on each corner, to cover the ends of the braid.

New Year's Eve

Beads, coiled wire and silver embellishments add a touch of sparkle to pictures of New Year's Eve celebrations. Lots of little ready-made ornaments are available to match this theme, so decorating the page is really easy. If the photographs are busy, keep the background simple so that there aren't too many things to distract the eye.

1 Cut a 30 x 15cm/12 x 6in rectangle of white card and mount all three photographs on it, cropping them a little if necessary to leave a narrow border of white between and around them.

2 Stick the panel of photographs in the centre of the black card. Punch four squares of black and white patterned papers and four squares of pale grey card and arrange them, alternating, down each side.

3 Wrap a length of wire around the dowel to form a coil. Stretch it to the length of the page, leaving 5cm/2in of straight wire at each end. Make a second coil to match.

4 Thread an assortment of small beads on to the wires. Use a generous amount as the wires are quite long.

5 Pierce holes at the the top and bottom of the layout where you wish to anchor the wires. Push the straight ends of the wires through the card and anchor them at the back of the layout with sticky tabs. Add the sticker embellishments to the plain grey squares.

6 Use a label maker to punch out a title for each photograph and the date on black tape. Stick the labels to the pictures and add the date in the corner of the layout.

materials and equipment

- craft knife
- metal ruler
- thin card (stock) in white and pale grey
- cutting mat
- 3 photographs, each 15 x 10cm/6 x 4in
- tape runner or glue stick
- 30cm/12in square sheet of black card (stock)
- black and white patterned papers
- 5cm/2in square punch
- fine silver wire
- thin dowel rod
- wire cutters
- small glass beads in assorted colours
- paper piercer or bodkin
- sticky tabs
- label maker
- black label tape

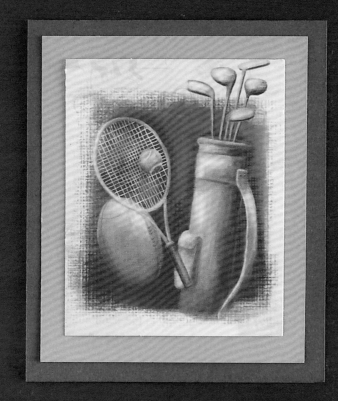

Sports

Whether your family members are active participants in sports, or fanatical supporters of a local team, sporting subjects make for rewarding layouts. This is a great theme for pages about children, where you can present them taking part in team games and school sports days, or showing off their daredevil skills on skateboards or bikes.

All kinds of games and sports make very satisfying subjects for scrapbooking pages, as they are all easily identified by the images and accessories associated with them, and there is plenty of strong colour in team strips, pitches and equipment. Add to these features the dramatic action shots you can capture in your photographs, and you can easily produce really eye-catching pages in this theme.

Cycling

This very simple double-page spread uses black ink trails to suggest the muddiness of a cycling trip in the countryside. Die-cut cog shapes and screw decorations reflect the mechanics of the bike.

materials and equipment

- black ink pad
- 2 x 30cm/12in square sheets of white card (stock)
- toy vehicle with rubber tyres
- sheet of metallic silver card (stock)
- craft knife and metal ruler
- cutting mat
- die-cut machine
- assorted cog dies
- matt silver paper
- 5cm/2in square punch
- photographs
- corner rounder
- glue stick
- paper piercer
- 5 screw brads

1 Brush the black ink pad around the edges of the sheets of white card to give the pages a "muddy" appearance.

2 Pat the ink pad on to the tread of a large wheel on a toy vehicle. Run the wheel across the card in different directions to create tyre tracks.

3 Cut two strips of metallic silver card 5cm/2in wide: these will form a band across the two pages. Using a die-cut machine, cut out a selection of cogs from the matt silver paper. Stick all the shapes to the strips, allowing some to overlap the edges and trimming them flush.

4 Punch details from photographs to create six square blocks. Round the two left-hand corners of the large photograph for the left-hand page, and the right-hand corners of a large photo for the right-hand page. Arrange all the pictures on the pages.

5 Position the silver strips under the photographs. Trim them so that the ends align with the pictures and round the corners. Glue everything in place. Pierce holes in the positions where you will insert the screw brads.

6 Push the brads into the holes and fold back the fasteners on the back of the pages to hold them in place.

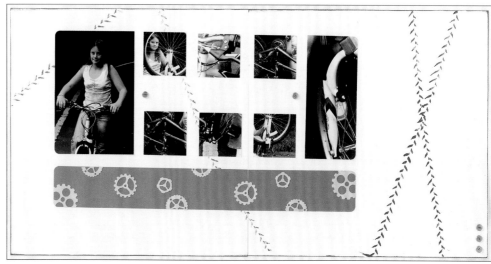

Basketball

The bright colours contrast with the black and white action photographs and the repeated circle motif clearly links with the ball game but also gives a sense of motion to the pages.

materials and equipment

- circle cutter
- thin card (stock) in lime green, turquoise and deep pink
- repositionable tape runner
- 2 x 30cm/12in square sheets of burnt orange card (stock)
- scissors
- eyelet tool kit
- letter stickers
- photographs
- 2 x 30cm/12in square sheets of chocolate brown card (stock)
- label maker
- black label tape

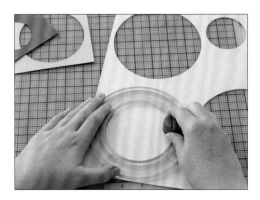

1 Cut out circles from the lime green, turquoise and deep pink card in assorted sizes. If you don't have a circle cutter to do this you can draw and cut out a number of templates or draw round plates and cups of various sizes.

2 Apply repositionable tape to the backs of the circles. This will allow you to move them around on the layout until you are happy with their positioning. Stick the circles to both sheets of burnt orange card in a random arrangement.

3 Allow some of the circles to overlap the edges of the sheets and trim off the excess with scissors. On the inner edges of the pages, stick the circles to one side and trim, then stick the remaining parts to the opposite page, aligning them accurately.

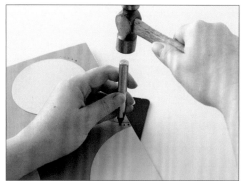

4 Use an eyelet tool to punch out small circles around parts of the large circles. If you have different sized punches try to use them all to add variety.

5 Create the title using letter stickers. When placing these, always work from the outer edge of the page towards the middle, which will sometimes mean spelling the word backwards, to ensure that each word is accurately positioned.

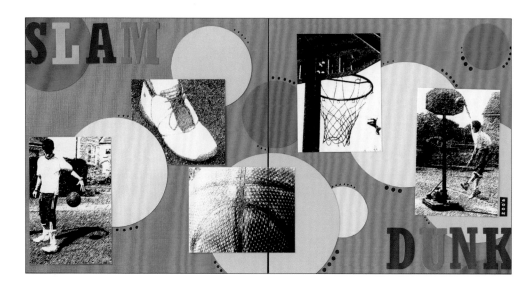

6 Position the photographs so that they overlap the card circles, taking care to avoid any of the punched circles.

7 Stick the finished pages to sheets of chocolate brown card, which will show through the punched holes.

8 Use a label maker and black tape to punch the date and stick the label beside one of the photographs.

Skateboarding

Grunge and funky colours go hand in hand with skateboarding, and this double page spread has plenty of both. Inks, fabric, curly paperclips and roughly torn paper combine to create a great background for these pictures.

materials and equipment

- 2 x 30cm/12in square sheets of turquoise card (stock)
- 2 x 30cm/12in square sheets of bright patterned paper
- thin lime card (stock)
- craft knife and metal ruler
- cutting mat
- ink pads in black and red
- hole punch
- roughly torn strips of woven cotton fabric
- "S" letter sticker
- die-cut "K"
- rub-on number "8"
- 4 round paperclips
- 4 photographs
- glue stick

1 Cut both sheets of turquoise card in half. Tear away a strip approximately 4cm/1½in wide from each side, tearing at a slight angle. Always tear towards yourself to expose the inner core of the card on the right side.

2 Moisten your finger and use it to roughen the torn edges of the card strips. Roll the edges back, without trying to do this too evenly. Stick the card strips on top of the squares of patterned paper.

3 Cut four strips of lime card 6mm/¼in wide and 30cm/12in long. Roughly ink the edges of each strip using the black ink pad, then glue to the turquoise cards, aligning the strips across the two pages. Punch pairs of holes to tie the fabric strips through.

4 To create the "S" for the title "skate", use the paper frame of a letter sticker as a template. Stick it gently to the layout (so that it can be peeled off later) and stipple through it using a red ink pad.

5 When the ink is dry, pull away the template. Add the die-cut "K" and rub on an "8" to complete the title.

6 Slide a paperclip on to the edge of each photograph. Arrange the photos at random angles across the centre of both pages and glue in position.

sk8

Skiing

Photographs of sunny days on the slopes demand pages with a touch of winter sparkle. This is a very simple layout, but the combination of snowflakes with silver patterned paper and an ice blue background gives a crisp, snowy look.

materials and equipment

- silver patterned paper
- guillotine (or craft knife, metal ruler and cutting mat)
- 2 x 30cm/12in square sheets of pale blue card (stock)
- eyelet punch
- tack hammer
- 24 silver eyelets
- foam brush
- acrylic paint in cobalt blue
- 6 sparkly snowflake buttons
- large white rub-on letters
- 4 photographs
- white card (stock), optional
- glue dots

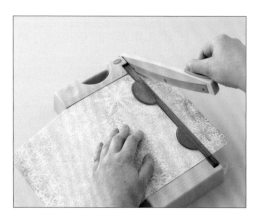

1 Cut 12 strips of silver patterned paper measuring 2.5 x 18cm/1 x 7in. If you don't have a guillotine, mark out the strips and cut them using a craft knife and metal ruler and working on a cutting mat.

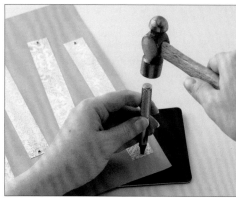

2 Lay the strips across the two sheets of blue card at uneven heights and angles. Use the eyelet tools and silver eyelets to attach them to the card at each end.

3 Using a foam brush, swipe a broad stripe of cobalt blue acrylic paint across the top left and bottom right corners of the layout. Leave to dry.

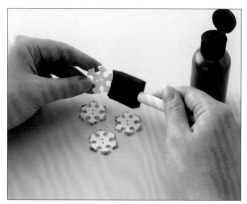

4 Dab the edges of the snowflake buttons with the blue paint to make them stand out more on the page.

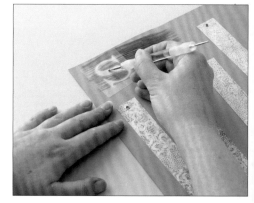

5 When the paint is dry, rub on the white letters over it to create the titles.

6 Print the photographs with a white border or mat them on to white card. Glue them at angles across the pages and stick on the snowflake buttons using glue dots.

Tennis

If you or others in your family enjoy getting to grips with the game, make this tennis court layout to celebrate your skills. You could personalize the page by using your own club colours for the background.

materials and equipment

- 30cm/12in square sheet of green card (stock)
- 2 x 30cm/12in square sheets of purple card (stock)
- craft knife and metal ruler
- cutting mat
- spray adhesive
- photographs
- white acrylic paint
- paintbrush
- alphabet foam stamps
- 2 purple and 4 green photo turns
- paper piercer or bodkin
- 6 dark green brads
- date stamp
- black ink pad

1 Cut two wide and one narrow strip of green card and glue them vertically to the purple sheets to make the background. Glue the photographs in position on both pages. Brush white acrylic paint on to foam stamps to print the titles.

2 On the right-hand page stamp the letters in reverse order from right to left so that you do not run out of space for the title. Take care not to overload the letters with paint or it will smudge. The words "game", "set" and "match" are used here.

3 Lay a photo turn over the edge of each picture and pierce a hole in the card through the eye of the turn.

4 Push a brad through the hole and fold the fasteners down at the back of the card to anchor the turn to the page.

5 Add the date in the corner of the layout using a date stamp and a black ink pad.

School sports day

Make a first school sports day special for your child by creating a spread in your album to celebrate their determination, whether or not they managed to win any prizes. Your choice of photographs can emphasize what a good time everyone had taking part in the fun races.

materials and equipment

- large square punch
- photographs
- large dinner plate
- pencil
- 30cm/12in square sheet of patterned card (stock)
- scissors
- craft knife and metal ruler
- cutting mat
- 30cm/12in square sheets of cobalt and navy blue card (stock)
- glue stick
- computer and printer
- pale blue card (stock)
- 2 metal sports embellishments
- glue dots

1 Use a large square punch to cut out three interesting sections from your photographs. Move the photos around in the window of the punch until you find the area you want. (If you don't have a punch, cut out the details using a craft knife and metal ruler, working on a cutting mat.)

2 Draw round a large dinner plate on the patterned card and cut out the circle using scissors. Cut the circle in half and position each semicircle at the outside edge of the cobalt blue pages. Cut two wide strips of navy card and glue them next to the semicircles. Glue a strip of patterned paper at the inner edge of the right-hand page.

3 Print the title "determination" in reverse on pale blue card and cut out the individual letters using a craft knife. The letters are less likely to tear if you cut out the centres before the outlines. Take your time and make sure the blade is sharp.

4 Glue the letters up the right-hand side of the layout using a glue stick. Position the whole word first to help you space the letters evenly.

5 Mat all the photographs on pale blue card and arrange them on the layout. Print a caption on pale blue card and add it to the first page.

Sports Day
Duncan's first sports day was great. They did lots of fun races and Duncan was determined to win them all. July 2005

6 Tie the metal embellishments together with a thin strip of pale blue card and attach them to the layout using glue dots.

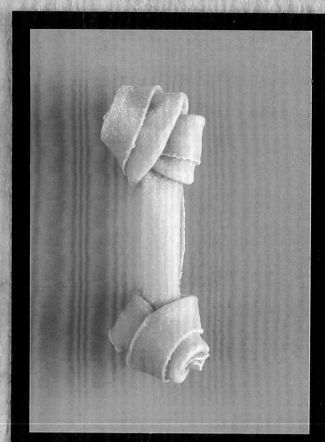

Family pets

Dogs, cats and other animals are important and much-loved members of many families. If you have pets, they're sure to feature often in your photographs of outings, celebrations at home, and fun and games in the garden, but it can also be rewarding to devote some special pages of your scrapbook to your animals, making them the stars rather than the supporting cast.

Animals' lives are far shorter than ours, and this is a lovely way to remember them in later years. Children usually have a special connection with their pets and love to look back at photographs of their antics, or to find out about pets that were around before they were born or when they were very small. Album pages can paint vivid pictures of your pets' lives if you include shots of them in youth and age, at play, at rest, enjoying their favourite toys and doing their party tricks.

My pet rabbit

Sometimes it's difficult to find the perfect ready-made embellishments for your pages, especially if you're working on an unusual subject. Why not make your own? Polymer clay is the ideal material with which to create easy small-scale pieces to decorate your album.

materials and equipment

- polymer clay in orange and green
- baking tray
- 2 rabbit photographs
- craft knife
- metal ruler
- cutting mat
- 30cm/12in square sheets of card (stock) in mid- green, dark green and lime
- spray adhesive
- large square punch
- green vellum
- tape runner
- rub-on faux stitches
- embossing tool
- wire cutters
- 3 rabbit buttons
- glue dots

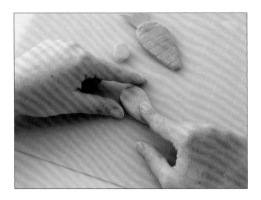

1 Mould a carrot shape in orange polymer clay and add some green leaves. Place the carrot on a baking tray and harden in an oven according to the manufacturer's instructions. Leave to cool.

2 Crop the photographs as necessary and mount on a large piece of mid-green card. Punch out three squares from dark green card and add them to the arrangement.

3 Create the left-hand border by layering a strip of torn green vellum with a narrower strip of torn dark green card. Glue the border to the background 2cm/¾in from the edge of the page.

4 In the 2cm/¾in gap use an embossing tool to rub on a line of faux stitches, taking care that they are straight.

5 Use wire cutters to snip the shanks off the backs of the rabbit buttons. Stick one to each dark green square using a glue dot.

6 Carefully tear green vellum into oval "lettuce leaves". Stick them overlapping at the bottom of the page.

7 Attach the polymer clay carrot near the lettuce leaves. Use a generous quantity of glue dots as it is quite heavy.

Folk art cat

The colours in these photographs of a favourite cat suggested they would work well with the natural blues, rusts and ochres characteristic of American folk art. This in turn inspired the simple embellishments of cut-out hearts and paper animal shapes, and the drawn "stitches" around the woodgrain panel, which are a reminder of traditional patchwork.

I On a background sheet of off-white paper, assemble a background collage using woodgrain design and complementary coloured papers. Cut out four triangles of patterned paper to go across the corners. Copy the templates of the cat, heart and dove motifs at the back of the book and transfer them to the back of the patterned papers. Cut them out using scissors.

2 Glue the collage elements on to the background paper. Leave a narrow border around three sides and a wider strip down one side on which to place the cut-outs. Glue the cut-out motifs in position. Attach the photographs to the woodgrain panel using brown gummed photo corners. Finish the page by drawing "stitching" lines around the edges of the collage with a black marker pen.

materials and equipment

- off-white heavy paper
- patterned papers in woodgrain and check designs
- craft knife
- cutting mat
- tracing paper
- pencil
- scissors
- glue stick
- photographs
- brown paper photo corners
- black fine-tipped marker pen

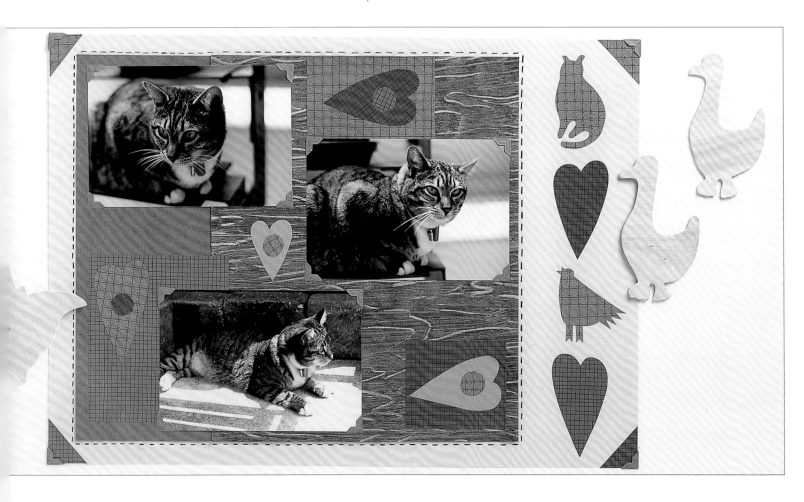

Best friend

Create a pet montage with cut-out photographs and conventional snapshots, and decorate the whole thing with fun paw prints and cute stickers. Using a combination of rectangular snapshots and cut-outs adds interest to the overall page, while the paw prints and stickers provide extra colour.

materials and equipment

- photographs of dog
- scissors
- 2 sheets of white card (stock)
- glue stick
- selection of children's stickers of dogs and puppies
- thin card in blue and green
- craft knife
- metal ruler
- cutting mat
- rubber stamp with paw print motif
- coloured ink pads
- paper towel

1 Decide on the general layout of the album page, then work out which photographs you want to use. Either make extra colour copies or, if you have enough, cut around some of the dog images with scissors. Arrange the pictures on the plain paper then, when you are happy with the arrangement, glue all the pictures in position. Decorate with stickers of other breeds of dog.

2 For the second page, mount the two main photographs of the dog on different coloured pieces of card, then add stickers all around the photographs to frame them. If you prefer not to place stickers directly on the original photographs, use copies.

3 Decorate both pages with paw prints, either stamping a border design or making random prints at different angles. Wash the stamp between colours and pat dry with a paper towel.

Bill and Ben the goldfish

Pet fish are quiet and unassuming compared with larger animals, but are often valued family members, so give them their own moment of glory in your album with a special page dedicated to themselves. The background paper used for this layout had a squared design, making it very easy to create a scrapbook "aquarium" for this friendly pair.

materials and equipment

- craft knife
- 30cm/12in square sheet of scrapbook paper
- gold glitter paper
- bubble effect paper
- metal ruler
- cutting mat
- square patterned paper
- spray adhesive or paper glue
- pencil
- coin
- goldfish photographs
- scissors
- star tags
- printed names
- blue ribbon
- card tags
- self-adhesive shiny paper
- plain self-adhesive alphabet stickers
- patterned card alphabet stickers
- PVA (white) glue

1 Cut a panel of gold glitter paper to fit at the top of the scrapbook paper and a panel of bubble paper to fit at the bottom. Glue both of them in place.

2 Cut a thin band of square patterned paper to go on top of the bubble panel and glue in place.

3 Draw around a coin on to the photos of your fishes, positioning it over their faces. Cut out the circles and glue one to each star tag. Print out the fishes' names, trim to size and glue one above each picture.

4 Trim the large photograph to fit the central panel, then glue it to the left side of the page.

5 Add short lengths of ribbon to the star tags and glue them in position on the right side of the page.

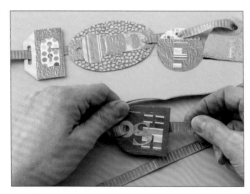

6 Decorate five tags in assorted shapes with pieces of self-adhesive shiny paper. Spell out the word "goldfish" on the tags with alphabet stickers. Thread all the tags in sequence on to a length of blue ribbon.

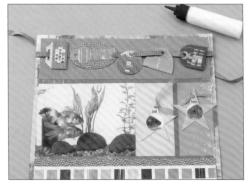

7 Position the ribbon across the top of the page then tuck the ends to the back of the page and glue them down with PVA glue.

Purry puss

This pampered fellow gets a very luxurious furry page to himself. If your cat is co-operative you should be able to get him to provide a paw print in paint with which to sign the page, but be sure to wipe the paint off his paw afterwards.

materials and equipment

- spray adhesive
- 30cm/12in square sheet of thin card (card stock)
- short pile fun fur or fleece
- scissors
- coin
- pencil
- thin card (stock) in red and green
- eyelet punch
- tack hammer
- gold rub-down letters
- 1cm/⅜in tartan ribbons
- PVA (white) glue
- 3 small swing tags
- gold paper
- glue stick
- photographs
- paw print
- narrow red ribbon
- collar bell
- 3 small gold safety pins
- thin red card
- metal ruler and pencil
- craft knife and cutting mat
- 4 photo corners

1 Spray adhesive on to one side of a sheet of card. Press the card firmly on to the wrong side of a piece of fun fur. Using scissors, trim the excess fabric from around the edges, as close to the card as possible.

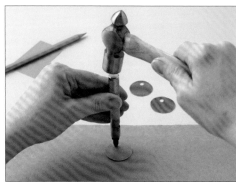

2 Draw around a coin on to red and green card to make discs, one for each letter of your pet's name. Cut them all out. Punch a large hole at the top of each disc with an eyelet punch.

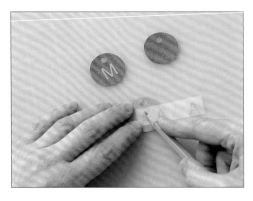

3 Rub a letter on to each disc to spell your pet's name, alternating the colours of the discs as you go.

4 Tie each disc to a length of tartan ribbon. Use PVA glue to attach the ribbons to the right side of the page, turning the raw ends to the back.

5 Glue three tags to the wrong side of a piece of gold paper and trim away the excess paper. Re-punch the holes in the tags with an eyelet punch. Glue a small photo of your pet to one tag, and a paw print to a second. Tie a small collar bell to the third with thin red ribbon.

6 Pin the three gold tags to the bottom left corner of the page, attaching them with small gold safety pins.

7 Cut a rectangle of red card measuring 1cm/⅜in larger all round than the large photograph.

8 Attach photo corners to the picture and and stick it to the mount, leaving an even border all round. Glue the mount to the page.

Prize-winning pony

If you have ponies that win rosettes for you or your children you'll want to honour their achievements by creating a special page. This is a very simple design using brightly coloured paper, with no other embellishments.

materials and equipment

- craft knife
- 30cm/12in square sheets of card (stock) in green and orange
- metal ruler
- cutting mat
- glue stick
- red, blue and yellow paper
- circle cutter or circular templates and pencil
- scissors
- photographs

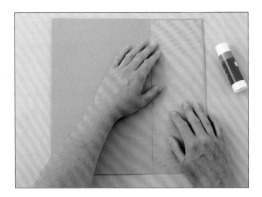

1 Cut a rectangle of orange card measuring 29 × 10cm/11½in × 4in and glue it to the right-hand side of the green card, leaving very narrow borders of green around three sides.

2 Cut three rectangles measuring 20 × 7cm/8 × 2¾in from red, blue and yellow paper. Glue them to the left side of the page, spacing them evenly, with the yellow at the top, then red, then blue.

3 Cut three triangles 20cm × 7cm/8in × 2¾in from red, blue and yellow paper. Glue them on top of the rectangles, placing red on yellow, blue on red and yellow on blue.

4 To make the rosettes, cut three large and three small circles of red, yellow and blue card. Glue the smaller circles on top of the large circles. Cut two thin rectangles in the same colours of each paper. Snip the ends diagonally to make ribbons. Glue the ribbons to the backs of the rosettes.

5 Draw a circle around each horse's head in a small photograph and cut it out.

6 Glue a horse's head in the centre of each rosette.

7 Glue the rosettes to the orange panel on the right of the page, with the red one at the top, blue in the middle and yellow at the bottom.

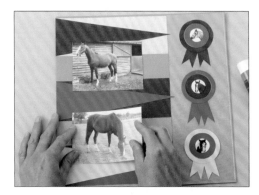

8 Glue two large horse photographs to the panel on the left side of the page, spacing the pictures evenly.

Travel

Trips and vacations are prime themes for scrapbooks: everyone's feeling relaxed, you have time to take lots of good pictures and – with luck – the weather's wonderful. If you're touring there will be new sights to see every day and new experiences to inspire you. Keeping your scrapbook in mind while you're away you'll remember to hoard lots of good-looking holiday ephemera, such as tickets, menus, hotel bills, little natural objects such as shells and pressed flowers, and maybe some exotic food packaging and foreign newspapers or magazines that you can take cuttings from.

Jot down plenty of notes so that you don't forget the name of that perfect beach or what you ate at your favourite restaurant. The more detailed your journaling the more memories you'll preserve, and the more fascinating your travel albums will be for you and your family in the years to come.

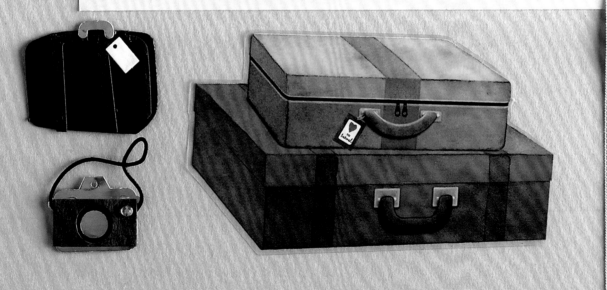

Beside the sea

A summer trip to the seaside is an intrinsic part of family life. The leisurely pastimes that make up a day's outing or a week's stay by the sea – paddling, swimming, beachcombing and building sandcastles – have remained unchanged over the years, and this album page brings together snaps of three generations of the same family having fun on the beach.

materials and equipment

- graph paper
- fine pen
- ruler
- A4 sheet of thin card (stock)
- craft knife
- cutting mat
- tracing paper
- selection of colour and black and white photographs and postcards
- watercolours
- fine paintbrush
- 30cm/12in square sheet of coloured card (stock)
- glue stick

1 Using the template at the back of the book as a guide, draw the postcard frame on graph paper, leaving margins of 5mm/¼in between all the shapes and 1cm/⅜in around the outside. Cut a rectangle of white card to the exact size of this rectangle.

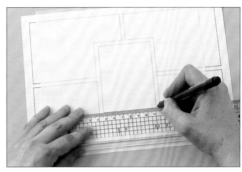

2 Trace each of the five segments on to a separate piece of tracing paper with a ruler and a fine pen. These templates will act as guides for selecting which images to use and where to crop them.

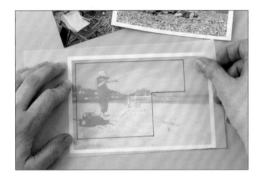

3 Place each tracing over your chosen pictures until you find a composition that will fit well within the outline. You may need to enlarge or reduce the photographs.

4 Black and white pictures can be hand-tinted with watercolour so that they blend in with the newer photographs. Use a fine brush to build up delicate layers of colour – without letting the paper become too wet.

5 Cut out the centre rectangle and one of the corner segments from the graph paper template. Draw around these segments on your chosen photographs and cut out around the outlines.

6 Glue the segments on to the white card rectangle, making light pencil guidelines to ensure that they are positioned correctly.

7 Photocopy and cut out other pictures that have not been used on the "postcard" then arrange these, along with the postcard itself, on the coloured card. Glue everything in place using a glue stick.

78342

Sightseeing in the States

The Stars and Stripes make a really colourful background, but this simple idea could easily be adapted using the flag of whichever country you have visited. The folded airmail envelope opens to reveal a mini-album of extra pictures.

materials and equipment

- dark blue paper
- craft knife
- metal ruler
- cutting mat
- 30cm/12in square sheet of white card (stock)
- silver star stickers
- pencil
- glue stick
- red paper
- 5 luggage labels
- photocopy of denim fabric
- hole punch
- photographs
- natural twine
- two airmail envelopes
- adhesive tape

1 To make the background flag, cut a 15cm/6in square of blue paper and glue it in the top left corner of the white card, matching the top and side edges exactly.

2 Stick 50 silver stars in nine rows to the blue square. For the first row space six stars evenly, starting 1.5cm/½in from the left-hand side, with their lower tips 2.5cm/1in below the top edge. For the second row position five stars between the stars of the first row.

3 Cut four strips of red paper 15 x 2cm/6 x ¾in, and three strips 30 x 2cm/12 x ¾in. Glue the strips to the white card to form the American flag, butting the short ones against the blue square, and leaving the same depth of white background between each horizontal strip.

4 To make the tags, remove the string from five luggage labels. Cover each label with denim paper and trim the paper to size. Make a new hole at the top of each label using a hole punch.

5 Trim a photograph to fit across the centre of each luggage label and glue in place. Tie a short length of twine through each hole.

6 To make the mini-album, fold two airmail envelopes into three. Tape the ends together to make a six-page album.

7 Trim the remaining photographs to fit the pages of the mini-album and glue them in position.

8 Glue all the tags in place on the flag page, then stick the mini-album in the centre of the lower row.

Irish castles

Ireland is known as the Emerald Isle, but as well as being green and lush, the rolling hills are crammed with impressive old buildings. The heraldic imagery and clear colours used to embellish this page reflect the country's historic sites and beautiful unspoilt landscape.

materials and equipment

- 30cm/12in square sheet of pale blue mottled paper
- craft knife
- metal ruler
- cutting mat
- 30cm/12in square sheet of dark green paper
- spray adhesive
- three photographs printed with white borders
- wavy-edged scissors
- tracing paper and pencil
- scissors
- thin paper, such as origami paper, in blues and greens
- glue stick

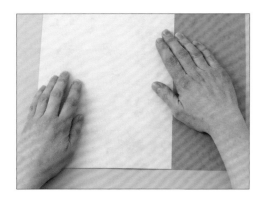

1 Cut a strip of pale blue mottled paper to fit across two-thirds of the green background paper. Glue it in place with spray adhesive, aligning the edges.

2 Trim the white borders of the photographs with wavy-edged scissors to give them a narrow decorative border.

3 Trace the fleur-de-lys template at the back of the book. Fold a small square of blue paper in half, with right sides facing, and transfer one half of the outline on to the wrong side. Cut out the motif. Cut a second fleur-de-lys from green paper.

4 Glue two rectangles of different coloured paper together to make a small square, then stick the blue fleur-de-lys centrally along the join.

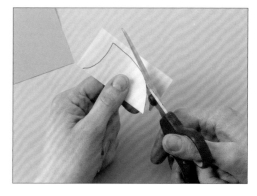

5 Use the shield template at the back of the book as a guide to cut out a small shield shape from pale blue paper.

6 Following the template, cut out a green shamrock and glue it to the centre of the shield. Glue the shield on to a square of darker blue paper.

7 Glue the three photographs in position on the page, overlapping them slightly so that the join between the two background papers is concealed.

8 Stick the two decorated squares and the second fleur-de-lys into the spaces between the pictures.

Trip to Japan

There is always something exciting about discovering a new country and its culture. Record your journey by collecting interesting ephemera as you travel; when you get back home, display it on a series of luggage labels.

materials and equipment

- patterned origami paper
- 30cm/12in square sheet of deep red card (stock)
- scissors
- spray adhesive
- photocopier
- old atlas
- emphemera including tickets, bills and wrappers
- luggage labels
- photographs
- fine permanent marker pen
- hole punch
- narrow black ribbon
- self-adhesive foam pads

1 Cut one sheet of origami paper in half, then glue one and a half sheets to the top left corner of the background card with spray adhesive, leaving narrow margins between them and around the outer edges.

2 Photocopy a map of Japan from an atlas, reducing the size as necessary to fit into the bottom right-hand corner, and cut out, shaping the upper edge in a gentle curve. Glue in place using spray adhesive and add two tickets overlapping parts of the map.

3 Remove the string from a luggage label. Place it over a photograph and draw round the edge with a fine waterproof pen.

4 Mark the position of the hole, then cut out around the outline and punch a hole at the centre top.

5 Cut a 20cm/8in length of narrow ribbon and loop it through the hole. Make one or more additional labels in the same way.

6 Small items of memorabilia can be displayed by sticking them on to plain labels. Larger pieces, such as a calendar page, can be reduced in size on a photocopier.

7 Tie all the labels together loosely in a bunch. Attach the knot to the top left corner of the card and then anchor the labels on the page with foam pads.

Spanish memorabilia

This collection of memorabilia from a vacation in Spain is attractively displayed in a practical way, with functional pockets in which to slip airline tickets, restaurant bills, postcards and other bits and pieces picked up during the trip. A photo-montage of attractive places can be made from a duplicate set of pictures to fill another page of the album.

materials and equipment

- craft knife
- metal ruler
- cutting mat
- 4 x 30cm/12in square sheets of red card (card)
- masking tape
- pencil
- eyelet punch
- tack hammer
- small nickel eyelets
- scissors
- tickets, stamps and other travel memorabilia
- bone folder
- glue stick
- assorted paperclips
- photographs

1 Using a craft knife and metal ruler and working on a cutting mat, cut out a 12.5cm/5in square from red card and tape it in the centre of one large square of card. Mark the positions for eyelets in each corner of the small square. Punch a hole at each marked point using an eyelet tool. Insert the eyelets through both layers of card. Tickets, pictures and travel memorabilia can be slipped under the small square.

2 To make a pocket, cut a larger square of red card and attach a smaller piece to it with an eyelet. Score around two adjacent edges of the square. Trim away the corner between the scored lines and fold in the edges sharply with a bone folder to make two flaps. Glue these to a large card square. Memorabilia, such as tickets, stamps and notes can be inserted in the flap pocket or attached to the pocket with paperclips.

3 For the photo-montage, use duplicate prints or make extra copies so that you can cut them up as necessary to make an effective composition. Arrange all the photographs and other pictures in a pleasing way on the last square of red card. Trim away any unnecessary parts of the photographs using a craft knife and a metal ruler, and working on a cutting mat. Once you are happy with your arrangement, glue all the pictures in place using a glue stick.

A day in the countryside

Machine stitching on card is a very quick way to add colour, pattern and texture to your page, and you can use a variety of stitches to real effect. This simple page uses fresh colours to echo the springlike tones of the photographs.

materials and equipment

- sewing machine
- light purple thread
- scrap card (stock)
- 2 x 30cm/12in square sheets of lilac card (stock)
- pencil
- scissors
- flower-shaped punches in two sizes
- light and dark purple card (stock)
- photographs
- glue dots
- pink rub-on letters
- embossing tool

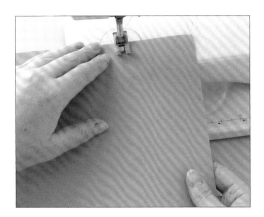

1 Thread the machine with light purple thread and do a test on spare card to get the tension right. Stitch slowly across the lower part of the page to create two gently waving lines. Align the starting points on the second page with the ends of the first lines.

2 Punch a selection of flowers from light and dark purple card using a large and a small punch.

3 Crumple the flowers to add texture. Flatten out and stick the smaller ones on top of the larger ones. Use glue dots to stick them along the lines of stitching.

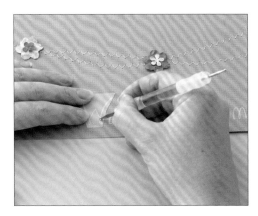

4 Double-mat the photographs on light and dark purple card and glue to the pages. Rub on the title lettering in one corner.

A weekend in Paris

This is an excellent way to combine a large number of photographs and your journaling on one page. The paper bag book contains pockets for mini-pages displaying more photographs as well as tickets, maps and other souvenirs.

materials and equipment

- guillotine
- photographs
- 30cm/12in square sheet of red card (stock)
- 3 flat-bottomed brown paper bags
- heavy-duty stapler
- selection of coloured card (stock)
- glue stick
- two-hole punch
- binder clip
- file tabs
- tickets, stamps and other travel memorabilia
- glue dots
- letter and number stickers

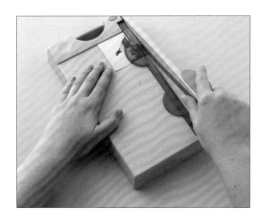

1 Using a guillotine, crop a selection of photographs into 6cm/2½in squares.

2 Arrange the photographs in a grid on the square card, using repositionable tape so that you can adjust them as necessary. Leave space for the title and the paper bag book on the right-hand side.

3 To make the book, stack the three bags together with the flat bottoms facing upwards and at alternate sides.

4 Fold the whole pile in half and make a crease at the fold. Staple along the fold to make the spine of the book.

5 Cut a piece of card to fit the height of the book and fold it over the spine. Glue in place using a glue stick. Punch two holes through the spine and insert the binder clip.

6 Cut out squares of card to fit the pockets created by the paper bags. Staple file tabs to the edges and fill the pages with pictures, ephemera and journaling.

7 Decorate the front of the book and place all the cards inside the pages.

8 Attach the book to the layout with a generous number of glue dots to support its weight. Use stickers to create the title and the date.

Celebrating the seasons

Though the seasons return to delight us year by year, no two days are ever truly alike, and nature is always ready to astonish us with its beauty. For photographers, the desire to capture fleeting effects of light and colour in the natural world is a powerful impulse, and successful attempts are well worth framing beautifully on your scrapbook layouts.

Pages with seasonal themes can make an album in themselves, perhaps highlighting your favourite landscapes or country walks, or tracing the annual round in your own garden. Or you can use them to punctuate more general collections of photographs, to place your family activities and celebrations in a seasonal context.

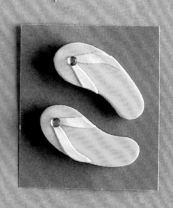

A seasonal mosaic

Photographic mosaic is a lot easier than it looks as long as you take your time and measure accurately before cutting up your pictures. Special sheets marked with a grid take care of all the spacing and lining up for you. This is a wonderful way to create an impressionistic image of seasonal flowers.

materials and equipment

- photographs
- repositionable tape runner
- cutting mat with printed grid
- craft knife
- metal ruler
- 30cm/12in square sheet white mosaic grid paper
- computer and printer
- thin card (stock) in white and mid-green
- scissors
- glue dots
- 5 metal charms with a garden theme

1 Cover the back of each photograph with repositionable adhesive. Be generous with this as it will make the cutting easier.

2 Stick each photograph to the cutting mat, aligning it carefully with the printed grid, and use a craft knife and metal ruler to cut it into 2.5cm/1in squares.

3 Reassemble the photographs on the mosaic grid. If you want any pictures to occupy blocks of squares, remember to allow for the spaces between the squares when calculating the size to cut.

4 Blend the edges of the photographs into each other a little, remembering to leave rectangular spaces for the titling as you arrange the pieces.

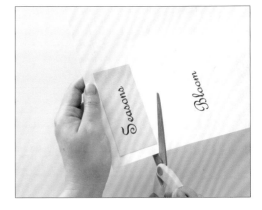

5 Print the titles on to white card. Carefully measure the spaces you need to fill on the grid and cut out the titles. Cut slightly larger rectangles from green card for the mats.

6 Mat the titles "bloom", "seasons" and "flower" and stick them in place in the spaces on the grid.

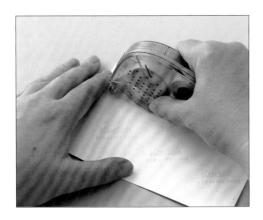

7 Use glue dots to attach the metal charms to the layout.

Bloom

Seasons

Flower

Spring in bloom

The bold colour scheme and geometric lines in this eye-catching picture of a tulip bed required an equally dramatic treatment. Red, green and white tracing papers, which have a translucent, matt finish, echo the colours of the flowers, and the spiral-petalled flower punch gives the finished page a strong, contemporary look. The white flower label bears the botanic name of the tulip species, but you could also use it to record the date or place where the picture was taken.

materials and equipment

- A4 sheet of white tracing paper
- 30cm/12in square sheet of green card (stock)
- glue stick
- 2 A4 sheets of lime green tracing paper
- scissors
- flower picture
- glue dots
- flower-shaped punch
- thin white card (stock)
- A4 sheet of red tracing paper
- fine marker pen or computer and printer
- pencil

1 Position the white tracing paper on the right-hand side of the green background card and glue it in place.

2 Position a sheet of green tracing paper so that it covers the lower part of the card and glue in place. Trim the edges as necessary so that they are all level.

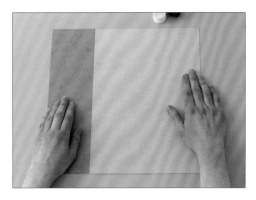

3 Position the photograph centrally within the lime green square and stick in place with glue dots.

4 Using the flower-shaped punch, make five flowers from white card and stick them down with a glue stick to form an evenly spaced row down the centre of the green rectangle on the left.

5 Punch seven red and seven green flowers from the coloured tracing paper. Arrange them in two rows across the top rectangle, alternating the colours, and glue in place with the glue stick.

6 Copy the plant marker template at the back of the book and cut out two green and two red shapes from the remaining tracing paper.

7 For the named marker, either cut out a white label and write a name across the centre with a fine marker pen, or print the name on white paper. Place one of the tracing paper markers over it so that the name lies centrally in the top part, then draw round it and cut out the shape.

8 Arrange the coloured markers down the left side of the page and the named marker at the bottom right corner of the photograph, and glue in place.

Glorious summer

This bougainvillea-clad house, replete with peeling paintwork and faded wooden shutters, epitomizes the languid days of high summer and is a reminder of a happy holiday spent on the shores of an Italian lake. A photograph taken in the garden of the adjoining villa shared the same colour scheme: this was cut up into squares to make a mosaic-style frame, and the background was chosen to harmonize with the flowers.

materials and equipment

- transparent ruler
- pink mulberry paper
- glue stick
- A4 sheet of pale green paper
- spray adhesive
- 30cm/12in square sheet of purple card (stock)
- marbled paper in toning colours
- craft knife
- cutting mat
- main photograph, measuring 17.5 x 12.5cm/7 x 5in
- two copies of a second photograph

1 Using the edge of a ruler to give a deckle edge, tear two strips of mulberry paper each measuring about 2 x 30cm/¾ x 12in.

2 Glue one strip behind each long edge of the pale green paper so that about 8mm/⅓in is visible. Using spray adhesive, glue the paper to the centre of the purple background card and trim the ends.

3 Using a craft knife and transparent ruler, cut four narrow strips of marbled paper, each measuring 6mm x 31cm/¼ x 12½in.

4 Glue two of the strips to the top and bottom edges of the card, to conceal the edges of the other papers. Glue the remaining strips to the side edges and mitre the corners neatly.

5 Glue the main photograph to the centre of the green paper, making sure that it lies completely flat.

6 Cut the other two photographs into 2.5cm/1in squares, using a craft knife and ruler and working on a cutting mat.

7 Glue these small squares around the main picture, alternating the light and dark tones to create a chequerboard effect.

Autumn colour

The fall in New England is world renowned for its glorious display of colour. Capture the hues of this "season of mists and mellow fruitfulness" with a special album page and make your own drift of dried leaves by using a special punch to cut shapes from duplicate pictures and toning card. As a finishing touch you could make a tiny luggage tag, using the leaf punch to make the hole and threading it with garden string, to record the date and location of your photographs.

materials and equipment

- spray adhesive
- 20 x 30cm/8 x 12in sheet of heavy cream tissue
- 30cm/12in square sheet of manila card (stock), plus extra for tag (optional)
- 3 autumnal photographs, plus an extra copy of each
- manila photo corners
- leaf-shaped punch
- glue stick
- coloured paper in matching autumnal shades
- self-adhesive foam pads
- garden string (optional)

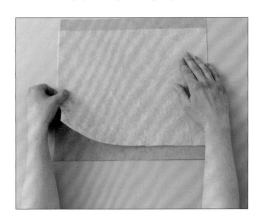

I Spray the heavy tissue lightly with adhesive and smooth it down across the centre of the manila background card.

2 Position the three photographs on the central panel and secure them using manila photo corners.

3 Use the leaf-shaped punch to cut out a few leaf shapes from the duplicate copy of the topmost photograph.

4 Scatter these around the edges of the main picture so that they appear to be tumbling down through the sky and glue them in place using a glue stick.

5 Punch more leaves from the side and bottom edges of the other two photographs and stick them down randomly around the pictures, matching the colours.

6 Cut a few leaves from the remaining tissue paper and fix these along the bottom of the card.

7 Punch a selection of leaves from the coloured card and arrange them in a drift, with the darker colours towards the darker areas of the pictures.

8 Overlap the leaves for a naturalistic effect and use foam pads for some, to give a three-dimensional effect. Add a manila tag tied with string if you wish.

Winter wonderland

Though it may be the most monochromatic of the seasons, winter is rich in texture: dazzling icicles, the beauty of snowflakes and the dense whiteness of fallen snow. These three snow scenes are mounted on a background flecked with gold and silver leaf, and brought to life with golden snowflakes, some handmade and others from a peel-off sheet.

materials and equipment

- three wintry photographs printed with white borders
- crinkle-edged scissors
- 30cm/12in square sheet of mottled grey paper
- spray adhesive
- tissue paper flecked with gold and silver
- scissors
- glue stick
- 12 small white paper fasteners
- A4 sheet of pale blue tracing paper
- gold pen
- sharp pencil
- peel-off gold snowflake stickers

1 Trim the borders of each photograph using crinkle-edged scissors to create a decorative, frosted border.

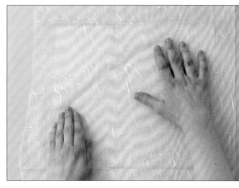

2 Spray the background paper lightly with adhesive and cover it with metallic-flecked tissue. Trim the edges flush with the card.

3 Position the pictures on the background, overlapping and angling them if you wish to create an interesting arrangement. Glue in position with a glue stick.

4 Insert a small white paper fastener just inside each corner of the three pictures.

5 Photocopy the snowflake templates from the back of the book. Place a sheet of blue tracing paper over the first snowflake and draw in the details with a gold pen. Trace the outline with a pencil, then cut out. Make another two or three snowflakes in the same way.

6 Arrange the snowflakes in the largest space on the layout and stick them down using a glue stick.

7 Finish off the design by sprinkling a few golden peel-off snowflakes across the page.

The four seasons

These four shots of family and friends enjoying country walks reflect the changing moods and colours of the seasons. Choose papers that echo these hues for mounting and add a border of punched motifs – the simple square format pulls together the different compositions and styles of the pictures.

materials and equipment

- light green, dark green, brown and ice blue paper
- ruler
- craft knife
- cutting mat
- pencil
- 4 seasonal motif punches
- thin coloured paper
- glue stick
- photograph for each season
- 4 sheets of tracing paper to match coloured paper
- 16 small coloured paper fasteners
- 30cm/12in square sheet of card (card stock)

1 Cut a 6in/15cm square from each of the coloured papers. Pencil in five equally spaced marks along two adjacent sides of each square.

2 Using these marks as guides, punch motifs around the two sides. Choose designs that reflect the season or location of each picture – such as a snowflake for winter and a sun for summer.

3 Choose a complementary coloured paper for each main square and stick a small piece behind each cut-out motif.

4 Glue each photograph to a piece of toning tracing paper, leaving a margin of at least 3cm/1⅓in all round.

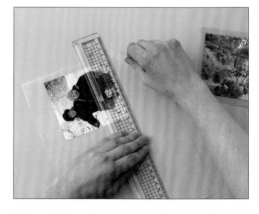

5 Tear the tracing paper against a ruler to create a narrow border with a deckle edge on all sides.

6 Glue the photographs to their respective backgrounds so that the innermost edges line up exactly.

7 As a decorative detail, attach a small coloured paper fastener to each corner of each picture.

8 Glue the four squares to the background paper, aligning them carefully.

TEMPLATES

Copy and enlarge the templates illustrated to complete your scrapbook album pages.

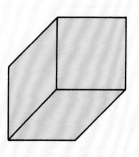

Making a kaleidoscope
p25

Decorating paper frames p28

Stencilling p38

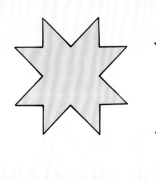

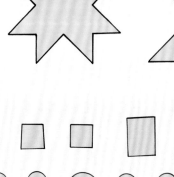

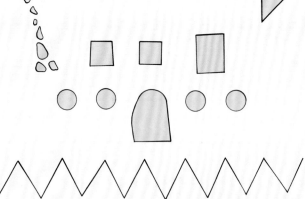

Stencilling p38

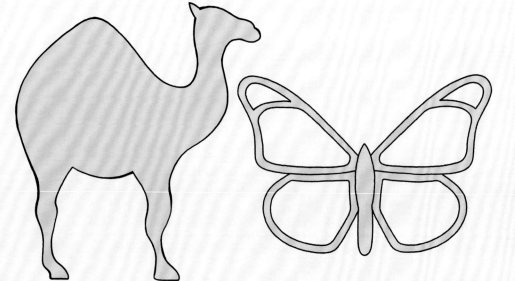

Paper appliqué p40

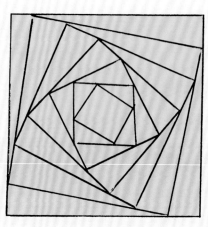

Iris-folding p48–9

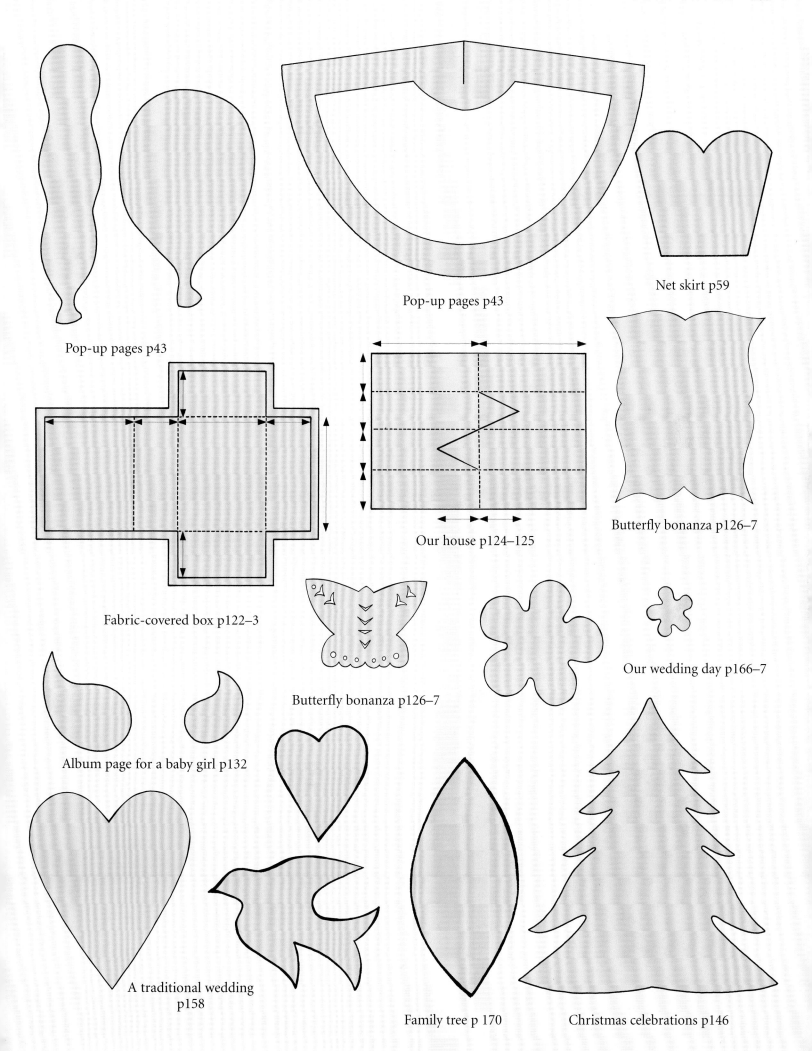

Pop-up pages p43

Pop-up pages p43

Net skirt p59

Fabric-covered box p122–3

Our house p124–125

Butterfly bonanza p126–7

Butterfly bonanza p126–7

Our wedding day p166–7

Album page for a baby girl p132

A traditional wedding p158

Family tree p 170

Christmas celebrations p146

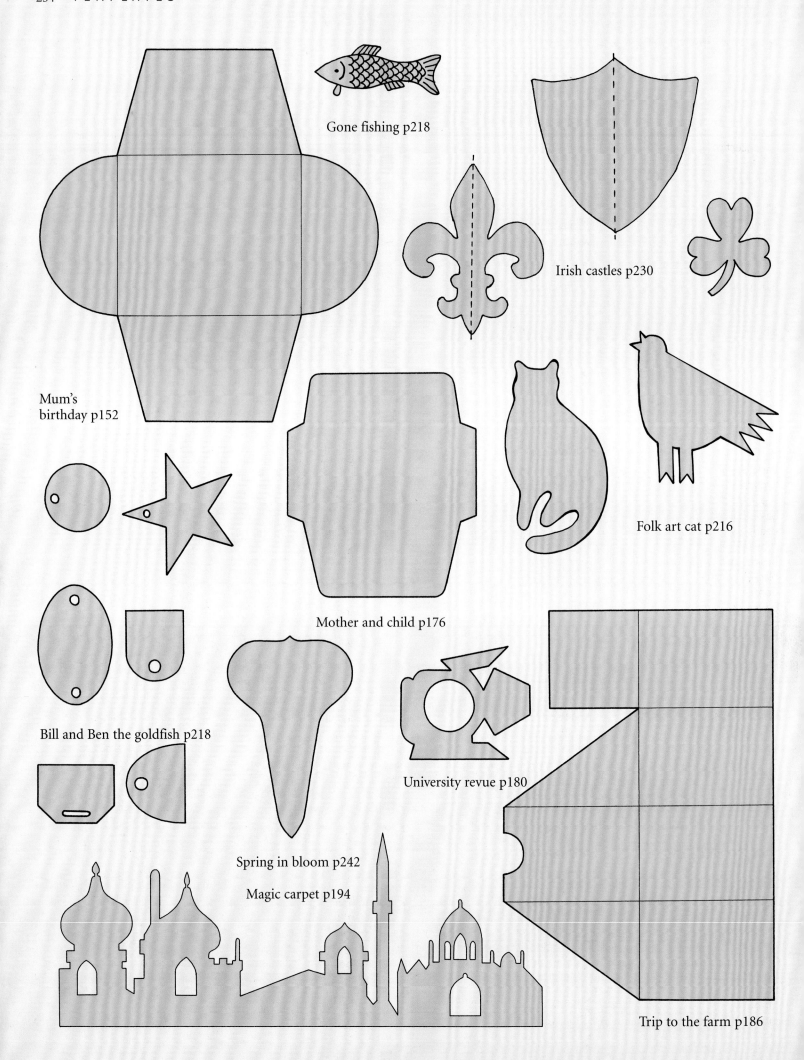

Gone fishing p218

Irish castles p230

Mum's birthday p152

Folk art cat p216

Mother and child p176

Bill and Ben the goldfish p218

Spring in bloom p242

Magic carpet p194

University revue p180

Trip to the farm p186

INDEX

ACKNOWLEDGEMENTS

Alison Lindsay p10, p11, p12, p13, p14, p15, p16, p17, p18, p19, p21, p22, p23, p24tr and b, p25, p29tr, p30 tint box, p31, p32, p33, p34, p35, p37, p39, p40, p41, p43, p42, p44, p45, p46, p47, p48, p49. **Penny Boylan**, p20t, p24tl, p28b, p29, p30l and c, p36, p38, p42cr, p108–9, p112–15, p120–1, p122 tint box left, p124–127, p130–1, p145b, p158–9, p184–5, p188–9, p216–7, p234. **Joy Aitman** p20b, p54tr, p57br, p132–3, p150–1, p154–5, p164–7, p174–5, p192–3, p196–7, p200–11, p214–5, p235, p236–7, p240–1. **Cheryl Owen** p50, p51, p52, p53, p54, p55, p56, p57, p58, p59. **Elaine Hewson** p64–75 and all other digital scrapbook pages. **Lucinda Ganderton** p100–1, p122 tint box right, p134–5, p138–9, p148–9, p170–3, p176–181, p194–5, p226–7, p230–1, , p232–3, p242–3, p244–51. **Mary Maguire** p102–5, p110–11. **Sue Hallifax** p106–7, p116–117. **Gloria Nichol** p122–123. **Marion Elliot** p136–7, p142–4, p152–3, p160–3, p186–7, p190–1, 218–23, p228–9.

Thanks also to May Taylor, Claire Longdon, Cher King, Pauline Craik and Sue Davies.

Thanks to the following suppliers: Hot Off the Press, Inc., Paper Cellar Ltd, Glue Dots, Efco Hobby Products, Arty's, Fibermark, Grassroots, Magic Mesh, F. W. Bramell & co Ltd, Cretive Memories, Junkitz, and Clearsnap Inc.